OSPREY AIRCRAFT OF THE ACES 123

Reconnaissance and Bomber Aces of World War 1

SERIES EDITOR: TONY HOLMES

OSPREY AIRCRAFT OF THE ACES 123

Reconnaissance and Bomber Aces of World War 1

Jon Guttman

OSPREY PUBLISHING

Front Cover

On 14 October 1918 Capt Rupert N G Atkinson of the RAF's No 206 Sqn led a bombing raid on a German ammunition dump at Sweveghem, in Belgium, flying de Havilland DH 9 D569 'A' built by Cubitt Ltd of Waddon, which had been assigned to him on 6 October. Clouds obscured the target just after Atkinson's lead element dropped its bombs, forcing the rear formation to target sidings and railway junctions outside Courtrai instead. As the squadron turned for home three Fokker D VIIs approached from the east. The lead German machine dived under the rear formation and the other two stayed 300 to 400 yards astern. Atkinson's bombardier, 2Lt John S Blanford, saw the lead Fokker climb to attack D569, and in a 1976 account published in the *Cross & Cockade Great Britain* Journal, he described what ensued;

'I alerted Atkinson and fired the usual red light signal. I watched the Fokker begin to climb again as he passed under our rear formation, and saw the observers in both of our formations open fire on him as he came within their range. At one moment I counted no less than five lines of tracers converging on him, but he still came on, climbing, and it became obvious that his intention was to attack Atkinson and me, while his pals distracted the attention of our rear aircraft. When he was about 70 yards astern of our aircraft, he suddenly pulled up steeply in order to get under our tail, my blind spot. However, he botched his attack, pulling up rather wide to starboard, which presented me with an easy target at point blank range.

'We opened fire on each other simultaneously. I gave him a good long burst with my right gun, hastily changed magazines, and let him have it with both guns – which meant 1200 rounds a minute – and my tracer appeared to be bang on target. I could see his tracer going past us, but I was too excited (and busy) to worry. Suddenly his nose dropped, and he fell away in a spin, emitting black smoke that in a matter of seconds turned to flame, so I knew he had had it.'

The Fokker reportedly crashed near Lendelede, and was also jointly credited to 2Lts H McLean and H P Hobbs, the latter of whom had hit it earlier before Blanford's bursts, in his words, 'gave him the *coup de grace*' and brought Atkinson's tally to five. German records credited Oblt Friedrich Röth, leader of *Jasta* 16b (whose personal markings here are hypothetical), with a DH 9 that day for his 28th victory (although all of No 206 Sqn's aeroplanes returned), but he was in turn brought down wounded in the foot, rendering him *hors de combat* for the remaining months of the war (*Cover artwork by Mark Postlethwaite*)

First published in Great Britain in 2015 by Osprey Publishing
PO Box 883, Oxford, OX1 9PL, UK
PO Box 3985, New York, NY 10185-3985, USA

E-mail: info@ospreypublishing.com

Osprey Publishing is part of the Osprey Group

A CIP catalogue record for this book is available from the British Library

ISBN: 978 1 78200 801 9
PDF e-book ISBN: 978 1 78200 802 6
e-Pub ISBN: 978 1 78200 803 3

Edited by Tony Holmes
Cover Artwork by Mark Postlethwaite
Aircraft Profiles by Harry Dempsey
Index by Alan Thatcher
Originated by PDQ Digital Media Solutions, UK
Printed in China through Worldprint Ltd

15 16 17 18 19   10 9 8 7 6 5 4 3 2 1

Osprey Publishing is supporting the Woodland Trust, the UK's leading woodland conservation charity, by funding the dedication of trees.

www.ospreypublishing.com

ACKNOWLEDGEMENTS

I would like to thank those colleagues whose invaluable assistance in the scavenger hunt for photographs and supplementary information have made this book what it is – Frank W Bailey, Christophe Cony, Everett R Cook, Jack Eder, Norman Franks, Jack Herris, David Méchin, Colin Owers, Alan Toelle, Aaron Weaver and Greg VanWyngarden.

CONTENTS

IN HARM'S WAY

Aerial reconnaissance in warfare made its debut on 2 June 1794 when the revolutionary French first used a hydrogen balloon during the siege of Maubeuge. Disoriented at the sight of what they regarded as a 'diabolical contraption', the town's Austrian besiegers nevertheless recovered sufficiently to raise their cannon in an attempt to shoot it down. History's first military aviator, Capt Jean Marie Coutelle, avoided this fate simply by letting out more cable until he had risen too high for their shots to reach him.

After the Battle of Fleurus on 26 June, which Coutelle's observations helped the French win, and the subsequent surrender of the Austrian garrison at Charleroi, prisoners of war testified to having heard their frustrated commander, Gen Friedrich Josias von Saxe-Coburg, curse the balloon, while summing up aerial reconnaissance's military value for all time by remarking 'there's a spy in that thing and I can't get at him to have him hanged!'

Observation balloons turned up in wars throughout the 19th century, and they were joined by aeroplanes as early as 1910 in Mexico. They also saw useful service during Italy's invasion of Ottoman Libya in 1911, the First and Second Balkan wars of 1912-13 and in the concurrent Mexican Revolution. However sceptical some conservative officers may still have been, all European powers had some aircraft on hand when Austria-Hungary declared war on Serbia on 28 July 1914, setting off a conflagration that would soon consume the world.

Arguably the first 'seal of approval' on the aeroplane came after the Battle of Tannenberg on 30 August, when Gen Paul von Beneckendorff und von Hindenburg declared that 'Without German aviation, there would have been no Tannenberg'. His striking endorsement was founded on a breakout attempt by the I Corps of the entrapped Russian Second

Antoine Paillard, whom *escadrille* mate Eugène Weissmann referred to as 'one of the great aces of bombardment', stands beside a Maurice Farman MF 7. A standard reconnaissance aeroplane for the French in 1914, it had been relegated to the training role by the time Paillard flew it in 1915 (*David Méchin*)

Army that was spotted by Gotha LE 3 Taube crews of *Feldflieger Abteilung* (FFA) 14 and, more importantly, their reports being accepted and acted upon by Gen Hermann von François, commander of the I Corps of the German 8. *Armee*. Their role in the overall victory was, in fact, grossly exaggerated, but the Germans encouraged that semi-fiction in the hope of keeping the enemy ignorant of their more decisive intelligence source – the Russians' own uncoded, intercepted radio and telephone messages. At the same time, however, the myth of the 'Tannenberg-*Flieger*' spurred the development of German military aviation until its vital importance became a reality.

The Allies, too, found reason to take the aeroplane seriously on 3 September 1914, when Sgt Louis Breguet, flying his own AG 4 biplane 60 miles over enemy territory with Lt André Watteau as his observer, confirmed reports that Gen Alexander von Kluck's 1. *Armee* had altered the course of its advance – intelligence that led directly to the critical First Battle of the Marne three days later.

BE 2s of the British Expeditionary Force (BEF) were also active before and during the battle, and likewise made a believer of Gen Sir John French, commander-in-Chief of the BEF. 'I wish particularly to bring to your lordship's notice the admirable work done by the Royal Flying Corps under Sir David Henderson', he wrote in a letter to Field Marshal Sir Herbert H Kitchener, Secretary of State for War, on 7 September. 'They have furnished me with the most complete and accurate information which has been of incalculable value in the conduct of operations'.

With the aeroplane's acceptance as an instrument of war came progressively more serious efforts to counter it. During the Siege of Tsingtao in September 1914 the Japanese gathered together nine aeroplanes whose task, in addition to reconnaissance and bombing, was to eliminate the lone Rumpler Taube, flown by Linienschiffsleutnant Günther Plüschow, which constituted the entire German air arm in China! They failed to do so before Tsingtao fell on 5 November – for his own part, Plüschow escaped, eventually making his way back to Germany – but by the end of the year numerous aerial clashes had occurred, involving everything from pistols and carbines to machine guns and even mid-air ramming.

The first airmen to set the standard for what would come to be called a 'fighter ace' did so before fighters even existed. On 2 November a Morane-Saulnier L two-seater parasol monoplane of *escadrille* MS23 was returning from a reconnaissance mission when its crewmen noticed a Taube following them. Taking umbrage, Sgt Eugène Gilbert slowed to let the enemy close to a distance of just 20 metres, at which point his observer – and squadron commander – Capt Marie de Vergnette de Lamotte fired 30 carbine rounds into it, causing the Taube to crash land in German lines.

Born in Riom on 19 July 1889, and qualifying as an aviator on 24 September 1910, Gilbert set several city-to-city speed records before the war, including a 3000-km flight in 39 hours and 35 minutes that won him the 1914 Coupe Michelin. On 18 November he encountered an LVG B I near Reims, and his mechanic, Soldat Auguste Bayle, punctured its fuel tank with a carbine, forcing it down in French lines.

On 10 January 1915 Gilbert and Lt Alphonse de Puéchredon attacked a Rumpler B I of FFA 23, Puéchredon's carbine shots wounding the pilot, Ltn Franz Keller, in the neck and arm and fatally striking the observer, Hptm Otto Karl Ferdinand Vogel von Falkenstein, in the heart. They also holed the aeroplane's radiator, compelling Keller to land. The French alighted nearby and administered first aid to Keller, who proved to have been a prewar admirer of Gilbert. The next day, in a gesture that would become commonplace, Gilbert dropped a message in German lines informing them of his opponents' fates, as well as a letter from Keller to his mother and sister.

Like a good many early French aces, Gilbert went on to fly single-seaters – in his case a Morane-Saulnier N firing a Hotchkiss machine gun through a propeller equipped with steel deflectors, with which he scored his fourth and fifth victories, before engine failure forced him down in Rheinfelden, Switzerland, on 27 June 1915. After escaping internment on 1 June 1916, Gilbert served as a test pilot until his death in a crash at Villacoublay on 17 May 1918.

Several other notable French fighter aces gained their first successes in two-seaters of tractor or pusher configuration, including Adolphe Pégoud, Georges Guynemer, Jean Chaput, Julien Guertiau, Georges Pelletier Doisy, André Martenot de Cordoux, René Pélissier, Charles Nungesser and René Fonck. Additionally, Russian ace Viktor G Federov scored the first three of his five victories flying Caudron G 4s with C42 over Verdun in March 1916 before flying SPAD scouts with SPA89, while his fellow countryman Eduard M Pulpe downed two enemies in Morane-Saulnier Ls of MS23 and three more in Nieuports prior to being mortally wounded back in Russia on 2 August 1916.

From this point onward, however, this account will focus on pilots and observers of both sides who scored five or more victories in tractor-engined reconnaissance and bomber aircraft. Aside from the fact that they are already covered in another Osprey book (*Osprey Aircraft of the Aces 88 – Pusher Aces of World War 1*), it might also be fairly stated that the Vickers FB 5s and Royal Aircraft Factory FE 2bs and FE 2ds in which most pusher crews achieved acedom blurred the distinction between roles by originally being defined as 'fighters' – a designation the British applied to those two-seaters, while referring to single-seaters as 'scouts'. In practice, the FB 5s and 'Fees' performed reconnaissance and bomber missions, but always with the understanding that a good pilot-observer team could give as good as it got against any aerial opposition. Their record of success, even as late as 1917, bears this out. It is no coincidence that several FE 2 units were later re-equipped with Bristol F 2B Fighters, which continued to combine reconnaissance and ground support with an aggressive readiness to engage enemy scouts (as recounted in *Osprey Aircraft of the Aces 79 – Bristol F 2 Fighter Aces of World War 1*).

Also worth a passing mention among the pusher aces is Capt Fernand Jacquet, the nearsighted but aggressive Belgian pilot who, thanks to some straight-shooting observers, was credited with four victories in Farmans and a fifth in the Farman-based Belgian-built Georges Nélis GN 2. In 1918 Jacquet commanded the Belgian *Groupe de Chasse*, at the same time seeking combat in tractor two-seaters such as the Sopwith 1A2 and the SPAD XI. While flying in the latter on 4 October his observer, Lt Marcel

One of World War 1's less successful reconnaissance aeroplane concepts, the ungainly Salmson-Moineau SM 1 had one transversely mounted radial engine using shafts and gears to drive two propellers for a three-man crew. Although the front observer and rear gunner had good visibility, the pilot did not, contributing to an epidemic of landing accidents (*Service Historique de Défense–Air*)

de Crombrugghe de Looringhe, forced a Rumpler down, followed by another two-seater on 6 November, bringing Jacquet's confirmed total to seven.

DIFFERENT APPROACHES

The changing exigencies of war led the French to adopt several approaches to reconnaissance, from scouting the frontlines to intelligence gathering deep in enemy territory and artillery spotting by units the French gave the prefix SAL (for *'Section d'Artillerie Lourde'*), and which German *Feldflieger Abteilungen* came to distinguish by an added parenthetical 'A'. Specialised aircraft evolved to carry out these differing missions, to which were later added close support and ground attack aeroplanes. Regardless of their particular niche, the French used a collective suffix for all their reconnaissance types – 'A' for *'Armée'*, as distinct from 'B' for *'Bombardement'*, 'C' for *'Chasse'* and 'E' for *'Entrainement'*.

Early reconnaissance work was primarily done by Farman pushers, tractor-engined Caudron G 3s, G 4s and G 6s or Morane-Saulnier L, LA and P parasol monoplanes. As those types became outdated, new candidates appeared in the form of slow, ungainly ARs, sturdy, reliable Breguet 14A2s and Salmson 2A2s, which boasted a combination of speed and durability – ideal for long-range missions.

Another approach to long-range reconnaissance was taken with the Caudron R 4 and R 11 and the Letords – twin-engined 'flying fortesses', which had machine guns fore and aft. These machines were designed to penetrate deep, gather the intelligence and, if intercepted, fight their way back. A short-lived addition to these lumbering gunships was the Salmson-Moineau SM 1, which used a system of shafts and gears to power two propellers from a single Salmson radial engine in the fuselage. An economic idea on paper, the SM 1 proved an unwieldy freak in practice, detested by its crews.

FRANCE'S MIXED BAG

Among the earliest distinguished French names in reconnaissance was a career officer who completed his rise to acedom in bombers. Born in Bordeaux on 14 March 1883, Joseph Vuillemin joined the army in 1904 and was a sous-lieutenant in the artillery by 1910. Switching to aviation in 1913, he was serving as an instructor at Reims when war broke out. Assigned to *Escadrille* CM (Caudron Monoplace), a training unit pressed into active service, Vuillemin flew scouting missions in Caudron G 2s over Alsace-Lorraine. In September his participation in the Battle of the Marne led to his being made a *Chevalier de la Légion d'Honneur*. When *Escadrille* CM evolved into C39, Vuillemin was given command of it on 13 January 1915.

On 26 June Vuillemin was promoted to capitaine and transferred to command C11 at Ancemont. On 26 August he asserted his possessiveness regarding airspace when he and Sous-Lt Guy de Lubersac attacked an Albatros over Vigneulles and were credited with 'probably' bringing it down. After another 'probable' on 9 September, Vuillemin and Lt Paul Dumas scored a confirmed victory, again over Vigneulles, as well as one unconfirmed three days later. These were followed by 'probables' on 19 September 1915 and 26 February 1916.

Lt Joseph Vuillemin (right), commander of *escadrille* C11 from 15 June 1915 to 16 October 1915, prepares to take Général de Brigade Antoine Nérel aloft in his Caudron G 4 from Villiers-lès-Nancy on 26 February 1917. Piloting one of these deceptively vulnerable looking machines over Verdun, Vuillemin was credited with downing a Fokker Eindecker on 30 March 1916 (*SHD-Air*)

Capt Vuillemin with Lt Paul Moulines (left), who succeeded him as C11's CO from 16 October through to 1 November 1916. Later serving on Vuillemin's *Escadre No* 1 staff, Moulines was killed in action on 26 March 1918 (*C Cony collection*)

By the latter date C11 was operating over Verdun, where armed French and German scouts were competing for mastery of the sky – more often at the expense of one another's two-seaters rather than each other's fighters. Although the French had formed specialised *escadrilles de chasse* for the task, Nieuport 11 N1313 was put at Vuillemin's disposal to escort his Caudron G 4s. Nevertheless, the only enemy scout credited to him during this period (a Fokker E III on 30 March) was shared with his observer Lt Paul Molines whilst flying a Caudron G 4.

On 26 June C11 was transferred to Villers-Brettoneux to support the British Somme offensive. Vuillemin was made an *Officier de la Légion d'Honneur* on 28 October, and on 11 May 1917 he scored his third victory over Sapigneule in a Letord 1A3 with crewmen Sous-Lt de Lubersac and Sgt Descamps.

Following more than two years with C11, Vuillemin left the unit on 16 October 1917 after having logged 1400 flying hours and 100 combats – this outstanding record earned him 11 army citations. The *Aéronautique Militaire* had greater plans for Vuillemin, for in January 1918 it expanded its concept of concentrating fighter and bombing assets over a given battle front from four-*escadrille groupes* to *Escadres*, each of which was comprised of three such groups. Thus, on 20 February, Cmdt Vuillemin was put in charge of *Escadre* No 12, made up of Breguet 14B2-equipped *Groupes de Bombardement* 5, 6 and 9 and *escadrilles de protection* R239 and R240 with Caudron R 11A3s that served as multi-gunned escorts for the bombers.

Not the sort to lead from behind a desk, Vuillemin frequently accompanied missions in a Breguet 14B2 marked with the red *cocotte* (paper horse) emblem of his old outfit, C11, often with Lt Charles Joseph Dagnaux as his gunner-observer. Born to a Protestant family in Montbéliard on 28 November 1891, Dagnaux had gone from artilleryman to aerial artillery spotter on 18 June 1915 when he joined MF63. On 6 February 1916 his Maurice Farman 11 was riddled by a Fokker, and although his pilot, Adj Jacques Loviconi, was unharmed, Dagnaux suffered three wounds that resulted in his left leg having to be amputated at the lower thigh. Learning to use a prosthetic, he returned to combat with C11 on 6 May 1917, often flying with Vuillemin. Lt Jean Mendigal was his pilot, however, when Dagnaux scored his first victory on 21 August.

This Letord 1A3, powered by two 150 hp Hispano-Suiza engines, was flown by Capt Vuillemin while commanding C11 at Hourges. He performed artillery spotting with it for the *2ème Corps d'Armée* during Gen Robert Nivelle's offensive in the Chemin des Dames. This was probably the aeroplane in which he scored his third victory over Sapigneule, in concert with Sous-Lt Guy de Lubersac and Sgt Descamps, on 11 May 1917 (*SHD B83-5641*)

While bombing the railway station at Waville on 21 January 1918, shrapnel struck Dagnaux in the neck, breaking an upper vertebra, but 20 days later he was serving on *Escadre* 12's staff at Vuillemin's request. Besides flying bombing missions with his old C11 CO, Dagnaux took flight training and finally earned his pilot's brevet on 2 September 1918.

On 26 April Vuillemin and Dagnaux destroyed a Rumpler near Montigny, killing Uffz Konrad Kayler and Ltn d R Hugo Schumann of *Fl Abt* 39. On 7 July Vuillemin and Lt Chalus downed a Rumpler C IV near Corcy. Vuillemin and Dagnaux downed another enemy aeroplane on 11 July, and on 4 October Vuillemin and Adj Elie Borel drove down a Fokker D VII over Semide, bringing Vuillemin's final tally to seven credited and eight unconfirmed aerial victories.

Credited with four victories, Dagnaux was made an *Officier le la Légion d'Honneur*. He remained active in civil and military aviation after the war, distinguishing himself in Africa with flights to Cairo in 1919 and Timbuktu in 1920. In World War 2 he commanded *Groupe de Bombardement* I/34. During a night reconnaissance to the Laon area on 17-18 May 1940, however, Dagnaux's Amiot 354 was struck by flak and crashed in flames near La Vallée-au-Blé. Pilot Lt Frank Frémond and radioman Sgt-Chef Lucien Regnault parachuted to safety, but navigator-bombardier Adj Maurice Lavolley and Lt Col Dagnaux, who was manning the upper gunner's position, were both killed.

After the armistice Vuillemin and his former bombardier Lt Chalus made several long-distance flights, including the first across the Sahara Desert on 18 February 1920, for which Vuillemin was made a *Commandant de la Légion d'Honneur*. Named interim commander of French aviation in Algeria in 1925, Vuillemin rose to the rank of *général de brigade* on 8 February 1933. After leading a 30-aeroplane flight to visit every major city in French-ruled Africa from 9 November to 26 December of that year, he was awarded the *Grande Croix de la Légion d'Honneur* on 13 January 1934.

On 24 June 1939 Vuillemin became *Général d'Armée Aérienne*. During World War 2 he received the *Médaille Militaire* for valour in combat on 17 June 1940 – a rarity for a general, but certainly consistent with his character. After actively serving throughout the war, Vuillemin entered the reserves on 14 March 1945 and subsequently retired, residing in Morocco until his death from cardiac arrest in the Lyon military hospital on 23 July 1963.

BACK-SEATERS TO THE FORE

When fighters were swarming around a reconnaissance aeroplane, barring a careless opponent stumbling into the pilot's line of fire, the two-seater's survival depended primarily on the coolheadedness and marksmanship of the observer. Several French 'back-seaters' attained ace status in the course of carrying out their duties.

One such individual was Charles Alexandre Bronislas Borzecki, who was born in Paris on 4 November 1881. Serving in army artillery from 1901 to 1903 and then rejoining on 4 August 1914 following the outbreak of war, he transferred to aviation as a photo section operator on 1 November, subsequently training as an aerial observer.

On 28 June 1916 Borzecki joined *escadrille* C43, and on 25 July he scored his first victory near Combles, killing Uffz Georg Röder and Ltn Friedrich Zilling of *Kampfstaffel* 11. Five days later Sgt Borzecki was

Charles Borzecki scored five victories as an observer, eventually learning to fly in the course of a long career in the French military (*David Méchin collection*)

Sopwith 1A3 N° 6, probably at N62's Chipilly aerodrome in November 1916, was photographed with its fuselage underside well besmeared with castor oil from steady use. Built by Sopwith, the airoplane was delivered clear-doped with khaki uppersurfaces and French cockades over the British markings, including on the fuselage – N62's fighting cock insignia had yet to be applied. Although the weapon had been removed from the aeroplane by the time this shot was taken, an earlier photograph showed a forward-firing Lewis machine gun mounted above the upper wing. From January 1917 with the delivery of N° 8, French 1½ Strutters were license-produced by Hanriot (*SHD B82-3085 via Alan Toelle*)

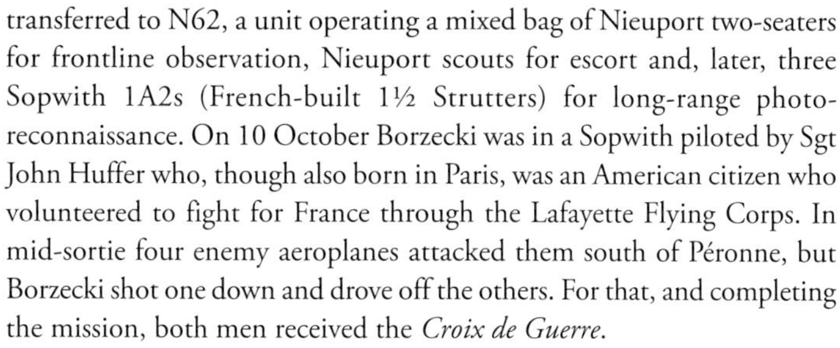

transferred to N62, a unit operating a mixed bag of Nieuport two-seaters for frontline observation, Nieuport scouts for escort and, later, three Sopwith 1A2s (French-built 1½ Strutters) for long-range photo-reconnaissance. On 10 October Borzecki was in a Sopwith piloted by Sgt John Huffer who, though also born in Paris, was an American citizen who volunteered to fight for France through the Lafayette Flying Corps. In mid-sortie four enemy aeroplanes attacked them south of Péronne, but Borzecki shot one down and drove off the others. For that, and completing the mission, both men received the *Croix de Guerre*.

On 23 November Borzecki and Sgt Gabriel Hébert were in Sopwith N° 6 on a photo run when they were attacked by eight German two-seaters. Borzecki shot one down and a second fell to Lt Pierre Lhuillier, who was escorting them in a Nieuport 17. A week later Borzecki was promoted to adjudant.

On 10 February 1917 Hébert and Borzecki were over Laon in 1A2 N° 22 when they were attacked by three German scouts that put five bullets into the Sopwith. Borzecki in turn sent one down to crash at Etouvilles, after which the Frenchmen completed their mission. On the 25th Borzecki and Brig Frédéric Fournier were attacked by three enemy aeroplanes, and again Borzecki downed one south of Pinon and drove off the rest. On 8 March he was made a *Chevalier de la Légion d'Honneur*.

Commissioned as a lieutenant by war's end, Borzecki went on to become chief of the photo section in Indochina in 1929, and commandant of Hanoi Aeroport in 1942, having by then also qualified as a pilot. Charles Borzecki had risen to the rank of *Grand Officier de la Légion d'Honneur* by the time he passed away on 30 May 1959.

Sous-Lt Borzecki was credited with two successes in Sopwith 1A2s with N62, but none in the SPAD XI in which he is shown (*Greg VanWyngarden*)

Another observer who learned to fly, Paul Homo was born in Arba, Algeria, on 10 April 1892 and entered military service on 11 December 1913. Commissioned as a sous-lieutenant on 6 April 1915, he served in the artillery until 1916, when he was assigned to Caudron G 4-equipped *Section d'Artillerie Lourde* 202 – an artillery-spotting flight

Photographed in the winter of 1916, a Caudron G 4 of *Section Artillerie Lourde* 202, attached to *escadrille* C53, sports the section's insignia of a red devil holding a cannon devised by the CO, Capt Julien Bertrand, who happened to be an artist. Adj René Pélissier and Sous-Lt Paul Homo were flying such an aeroplane when they shot down a Fokker Eindecker over St Christ on 29 July 1916 – the first of an eventual eight victories for Pélissier (six scored in fighters with SPA155) and five for Homo (*SHD B91-4225*)

attached to C53. Homo was on such a mission, with Adj René Pélissier as his pilot, on 29 July when they were attacked by a Fokker Eindecker over St Christ – the German scout was duly shot down. While flying a Farman F 40 on 22 October they were attacked by an Aviatik, which Homo again despatched between Villers-Carbonnel and Brie. Pélissier would go on to be credited with six more victories as a fighter pilot with SPA155.

Homo was transferred to C225 in March 1917, and he had Lt Francisque Floret as his pilot when he fought the action described in his *Chevalier de la Légion d'Honneur* citation on 11 June;

'During the course of regulating artillery, on 2 May 1917 he was attacked by six German aeroplanes, but put them to flight after downing two, returning with his aeroplane riddled with bullets.'

Leaving C225 on 8 June, Homo was promoted to lieutenant on 6 July and on 12 August he began flight training at Le Crotoy, earning his pilot's brevet on 11 October. In January 1918 he was assigned to Sop207, but in February he was given command of Br235. On 12 July Homo scored his fifth victory when he and Sous-Lt Pierre Guerin, in concert with three aces from SPA154 (Sous-Lts Michel Coiffard and Robert Waddington and MdL Jacques Ehrlich), sent an Albatros D Va down in flames west of Bois de Vrigny, killing Uffz Karl Röttgen of *Jasta* 39.

Remaining in service into World War 2, Homo was a colonel and a *Commandeur de la Légion d'Honneur* when he retired in 1954. He died in Roquencourt (Yvelines) on 20 April 1968.

France's oldest ace had experienced enough adventure to fill a book before he ever saw an aeroplane! Born in Brussels on 17 March 1874, Adolphe Aloïs de Gonzague Marie Hubert Ghislain du Bois d'Aische was the scion of Walloon nobility whose genealogy dated back to at least the 15th century. He was a wilful boy, however, and when his father, Count Adrien du Bois d'Aische, opposed his wish to study engineering, and then

Sous-Lts Homo (left) and Francisque Floret of C225 pose for the camera after the action described in Homo's *Chevalier de la Légion d'Honneur* citation on 11 June 1917. 'During the course of regulating artillery, on 2 May 1917, he was attacked by six German aeroplanes, but put them to flight after downing two, returning with his aeroplane riddled with bullets' (*C Cony collection*)

Sgt Adolphe du Bois d'Aische and friend after the former scored his sixth victory to become France's most elderly ace (*C Cony collection*)

sought to arrange a 'proper' bride for him, it drove Adolphe to travel to the Belgian Congo. On 4 September 1904 he enlisted in the French Foreign Legion, learning German from his many Teutonic comrades-in-arms and acquiring French citizenship by the time he mustered out. In France he fell in love with and married Constance Catesson, with whom he settled in Paris and took up a career in engineering in 1914.

When war broke out du Bois d'Aische enlisted in the infantry and fought at the Marne, the Argonne and in Vauquois. Wounded on 4 April 1915, he transferred to the *Aéronautique Militaire* on 15 July and served as a mechanic at the Avord aviation school, before training to be an observer-gunner at Cazaux. On 6 April 1916 Cpl du Bois d'Aische was assigned to F71. Based at Commercy, near St Mihiel, and equipped with Farman F40s, the unit performed reconnaissance duties for the *VIIIe Corps d'Armée* around Verdun.

On 22 May 1916 du Bois d'Aische was undertaking a photo-reconnaissance mission over the Varninay area with pilot Lt Pierre Théodore Weiss when, he recounted, 'for the first time I had the joy to see Boches. There were three. My pilot, in manoeuvring, found a means of tricking them by feigning flight. Soon, one of the Albatros, giving in to the trap, abandoned his comrades to give chase to us. That was what we were waiting for. Once we saw he was sufficiently far from the others, in a brusque dive we turned into him and at 50 metres I had the pleasure to enter a short combat and to see my adversary crash to earth'.

After Verdun the *escadrille* moved twice, ending up at Sainte-Ménehould on 23 January 1917 to support Gen Robert Nivelle's spring offensive along the Chemin des Dames. In April F71 received seven Salmson-Moineau SM 1s and suffered four aircrew wounded. This spell of intense action was capped off on 14 May by the loss of SM 1 N° 134 and its crew, Cpl Jean Hiribarne, Sous-Lt Hippolyte Mercier and Sol François Rafflin, to Ltn Hermann Pfeiffer of *Jasta* 9.

In early June Sopwith 1A2s replaced the SM 1s, and du Bois d'Aische and his pilot Brig Jacques Fontaine were in one on the 3rd when they spotted five German fighters above them. 'The first Boche dived and, shot at 30 metres, continued his vertiginous dive right into the ground', du Bois d'Aische reported. 'The second followed the same route and, nicely hit, likewise crashed in a forest'. A third German attacked, only to be struck and forced to land. The remaining two retired. Fontaine and du Bois d'Aische were credited with one of the fighters, which crashed north of Laffaux.

In July F71 got its first AR 1s. Conceived by Lt Col Émile Dorand of the *Section Technique de l'Aéronautique* and designed by Capt Georges Le Pére, the *Avion de Reconnaissance* AR 1 began flight-testing in September 1916 and entered service in April 1917. Powered by a 160 hp Renault 8Gd engine, its maximum speed was 92 mph.

On 24 July F71 despatched MdL Antoine Clément and Lt Jean Baptiste Reibell on a photo-reconnaissance mission 15 km behind German lines. Three other ARs acted as escorts, crewed by Sgt Christian Boullaire and Cpl Robert Lahémade on the right, Cpls Henri Bétis and du Bois d'Aische on the left and Adj Roger Pons and Sgt Adolphe Couture to the rear.

The AR 1 crewed by Cpls Henri Bétis and du Bois d'Aische after crashing in French lines on 24 July 1917. Although they were credited with downing two of their assailants, Bétis died of his injuries. His observer du Bois d'Aische somehow emerged from the wreckage unhurt (*C Cony collection*)

When the diamond formation entered enemy territory anti-aircraft fire slackened and, as the French expected, seven Albatros and Roland fighters came at them from above, behind and the left. In moments Couture was mortally struck and a wounded Pons, covered by Boullaire and Lahémade, force landed in Allied lines.

Meanwhile, du Bois d'Aische was manning his Lewis gun, shooting one assailant down in flames and sending another crash-landing near Cernay-en-Dormois. Bétis, however, was hit in the stomach and the AR's fuel tank was riddled. 'Falling from spin to spin all the way to the third line of

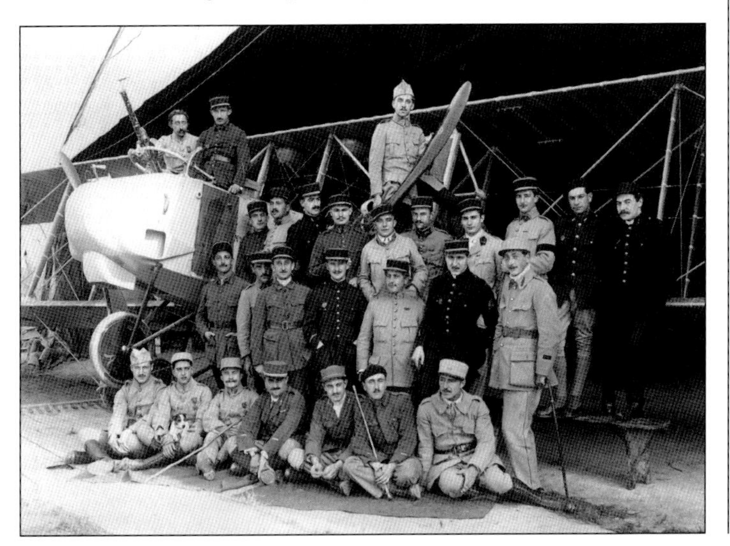

F71 personnel pose before one of their Letord 1A3s at Sainte-Ménehould aerodrome, with a wooden panel added bearing the *escadrille's* parrot emblem and Sgt du Bois d'Aische perched in the front observer's pit. He was probably in this aeroplane when he scored his last two victories on 22 September 1917 (*C Cony collection*)

trenches', du Bois d'Aische recalled, 'I coldly considered myself to have had it'. Bétis, however, maintained just enough control to crash land in Allied territory. Du Bois d'Aische emerged unhurt but Bétis died of his wounds three days later. Curiously, there were no German claims for two-seaters that day, but *Jasta* 9 recorded the death of Ltn Oskar Dänkert at Pont-à-Chin. Credited with both enemy fighters, du Bois d'Aische was promoted to sergent.

Later that summer Letord 1A3s were issued to F71. On 22 September Brig Fontaine was flying one of the triplaces over Cernay-en-Dormois, with du Bois d'Aische up front taking 20 photographs and Lt Marcel Meunier manning the rear gunner's pit, when three Albatros scouts dived on them. 'The first soon arrived at a good distance, and at between 30 and 40 metres three or four bullets sent him right to the ground in flames', du Bois d'Aische wrote. The remaining two Germans retired.

Moving on to Vouziers, the Letord crew shot up two troop trains before returning to find a large German two-seater directing fire on French artillery positions. Descending, Fontaine and his crew engaged the aeroplane and sent it crashing in German lines. Cited for his fifth and sixth victories and awarded the *Médaille Militaire*, du Bois d'Aische had joined the pantheon of French aces at the age of 43, but he wanted more – he requested a waiver on the *Aéronautique*'s 30-year-old ceiling on fighter pilot training. Leaving F71 on 16 December 1917, du Bois d'Aische trained at Cazaux and Istres and received his brevet on 25 June 1918. While at the *Groupe des Divisions d'Entrainement* at Le Bourget-Dugny, however, he was injured in a SPAD crash on 3 October. He was demobilised at Chartres on 10 December.

Du Bois d'Aische spent the inter-war years in civil aviation. World War 2 found him residing in his wife's home town of Saint-Quay-Portrieux, where his fluency in German led to his working for the Nazi occupation forces as an interpreter and administrator – until they discovered that he was secretly warning the French Resistance of every upcoming arrest. Imprisoned in a fortress, he defied all manner of interrogation until 1944, when he was liberated. Adolphe du Bois d'Aische served as a municipal councillor thereafter, dying on 7 October 1958, aged 84.

Lts Albert Mézergues and Anselme Marchal reunite at the *Aéro Club de France* on 4 April 1918, shortly after their escape from imprisonment in Germany. Marchal gained fame for flying over Berlin in June 1916 and dropping pamphlets on the German capital. He attempted to continue his long flight from Nancy across Germany to Russian lines but was forced to land in enemy territory and was duly taken prisoner (*C Cony collection*)

Breguet Bombers

By 1915 French Farmans, Voisins and Caudrons were carrying out bombing missions from the frontlines to the industrial centres of the Saar region. A handful of future aces got their starts in such aeroplanes, but it was not until the introduction of the rugged, reliable Breguet 14B2 that pilots and bombardiers achieved scores of five or more during massed sorties in the face of persistent aerial opposition.

Matching the Breguet for durability, Lt Albert Edmond Mézergues entered combat in 1914 and claimed his first two victories flying Voisins with V21 on 23 and 27 March 1916. He successively served in V90, N79 and Sop123, before being shot down and taken prisoner while in Sop129 on 22 August 1917. Mézergues escaped on 26 February 1918 and was then assigned to *Groupe de Bombardement* (GB) 4 on 22 May, as commander of Br131. By the end of the war Mézergues had logged 129 bombing sorties, 65 photo-reconnaissance sorties, 11 artillery spotting sorties and 45 surveillance flights. He had

Capt Mézergues, CO of Br131, stands at left beside Breguet 14B2 N° 4070 and an unidentified squadronmate. Mézergues' wartime record in six different *escadrilles* included 107 bombing sorties, 65 photo-reconnaissance missions, 11 artillery-spotting *réglages* (controlling the fall of shot), 45 surveillance missions and seven aerial victories (*SHD B83-5666*)

also received credit for seven victories, the last two of which were achieved in September 1918. Mézergues' decoratons included the *Chevalier de la Légion d'Honneur* and the *Ordinul Coruana României*. Serving on postwar, Mézergues was killed during a mission in Spanish Morocco on 15 May 1925.

Serving alongside Mézergues in GB4 was the team of Capt Jean-François Jannekeyn and Lt Eugène Weismann. Jannekeyn was born in Cambrai on 16 November 1892, and he served in the *4e Régiment de Cuirassiers* before transferring to aviation, rising to the rank of capitaine and being given command of Br132 on 23 May 1918.

Born the son of a Parisian physician on 18 March 1896, Eugène Weismann was spending Passover at the villa of an uncle near Le Mans in 1909 when a nearby field was cordoned off and a visiting aviator offered to take up the lightest weight volunteer as a passenger. Thus, 13-year-old Weismann got his introduction to flight seated alongside Wilbur Wright. With the outbreak of war, Weismann dropped out of college to enlist on 25 September 1914. Joining the *28e Régiment d'Infanterie* in October, he was wounded at Berry-au-Bac in November and at Artois in May 1915. During his second convalescence Weismann took officer training at Saint-Cyr, then rejoined his unit at Verdun. Whilst opposing a German assault on 31 May 1916 Aspirant Weismann's feet were shattered by a grenade blast and had to be amputated the next day.

Aided by his father, Weismann learned to walk on two prosthetics. Following aerial gunnery training at Cazaux he became an instructor at Avord until his request to re-enter combat was approved on 4 October 1917. On 22 November he was assigned to Sop132 at Luxeuil-les-Bains, which re-equipped with Breguet 14B2s on 25 January 1918 and was subsequently amalgamated into GB4. Weismann was temporarily

Sous-Lt Eugène Weismann and Capt Jean-François Jannekeyn pose beside Breguet 14B2 N° 4231 of Br132, showing the *escadrille's* 'Annamite dragon' pennant. The duo was jointly credited with five victories – four in one harrowing mission – but followed divergent paths during World War 2 (*SHD B76-1337*)

commissioned a sous-lieutenant on 19 April. On 4 May he and his pilot, Adj René Germain, were credited with an enemy aeroplane over Chauny, and on 2 June he, Germain and other crews from his formation were jointly credited with a German fighter destroyed.

Then came the final German effort along the Marne on 15 July, after which Weismann said 'we did an enormous amount of work, flying two or three missions per day. Losses were considerable. It was above all the Breguet that stopped the German infantry. However, to attack these enemy breakthroughs one had to descend extremely low – down to 15-20 metres – before loosing off the bombs and machine gunning them'.

A few days later Sous-Lt Antoine Paillard said to Weismann, 'Since it's such a beautiful day, what would you say to taking a little trip?' The jaunt Paillard had in mind involved their taking a Breguet with as much fuel, ammunition and bombs as it could carry across the lines at an altitude of just seven or eight metres and flying 50 km into German territory. Here, they found a horsedrawn supply column, which they hit with 24 bombs before strafing it. After an intense 20 minutes of action the column had been all but annihilated.

Antoine Joseph Henri Louis Paillard, whom Weismann described as 'one of the great aces of bombardment', was born in Sainte-Gemmes-d'Andigné on 23 August 1897. A mechanic when war broke out, he enlisted in aviation on 29 April 1915, earned his pilot's brevet on 4 January 1916 and was assigned to VC111 on 14 March. Sopwiths replaced the unit's Voisins exactly one year later.

At 2330 hrs on 6 July 1917 Adj Paillard and Sgt Maxime Gallois took off in single-seat Sopwith 1B1s to bomb the Krupp factory at Essen, while Lt Jean Ardisson de Perdiguier hit Koblenz and Sgt Georges Durand struck Trier. The nocturnal raid was the precursor to a larger, three-hour

Capt Mézergues chats with another pilot, who appears to be Lt Charles Nungesser of SPA65, in front of Breguet 14B2 1818, Nº 1. At this time Br131 bomb-toting red chimera insignia was highlighted in white on the vertical stabiliser and the unit's aeroplanes also had their cowlings and wheel hubs painted in alternating red and white secondary décor (*SHD B89-499*)

mission the following night, which the Germans reported scored 48 bomb hits and caused 105,128 marks worth of damage, although nobody was killed. The sole French loss was Paillard, who, suffering from disorientation and engine trouble, was forced to land in the Netherlands, where he and his Sopwith were interned. On 4 November, however, he escaped and made his way back to France. Sous-Lt Paillard joined Br132 on 22 March 1918, and on 31 May he and Sous-Lt Adolphe Calbet were credited with an enemy aeroplane destroyed.

Capt Jannekeyn and Sous-Lt Weismann were teamed up on 22 August when they fought off several attackers, one of which was credited to them. Their opponents may have been from *Jasta* 74, whose commander, Oblt Theodor Cammann, came down wounded, while Off Stv Willi Hippert claimed a Breguet that went unconfirmed.

Br132's most harrowing fight occurred on 14 September when GB4 bombed the railhead at Conflans in support of the American St Mihiel offensive. At 0830 hrs 28 Breguets of Br131, Br132 and Br134 took off, with five Caudron 11A3s of R46 as escorts. 'It was a pig of a day', Weismann recalled, 'with an enormous wind that blew from west to east. The rendezvous was to be made over a small bell tower, the bombing to be done at 3000 metres. When we arrived Br134 wasn't there and Br131 had not waited for us. Jannekeyn ordered, "We're going in"'.

Over Conflans-Jarny the 14 Breguets came under attack by *Jasta* 13, led by high-scoring ace Ltn Franz Büchner. Meanwhile, *Jasta* 65 engaged the escorts, two Caudrons falling victim to Ltn Wilhelm Frickart and Vzfw Josef Hohly. 'Extraordinarily, the aerial combat lasted 45 minutes', Weismann recalled. 'We did our bombardment of the station, but when we wanted to return home our aeroplanes faced a strong 100 km per hour wind – we normally ran at 180 km per hour full out. We didn't advance and lost a lot of crews'.

Br131 had claimed four Fokkers – one of which was credited to Capt Mézergues – while losing one aeroplane, apparently to Büchner. Br132 lost four machines, two to Büchner, one to Ltn Werner Niethammer and one to Ltn d R Grimm, while also claiming four Fokkers – *Jasta* 13 lost no pilots, however – shares of which were jointly credited, among others, to Jannekeyn and Weismann, as well as Paillard and his bombardier, Sgt Hincelin, although a later confirmation statement suggests that in fact each of the four were singly earned victories. If the shared victories are accepted, they would bring Paillard's and Jannekeyn's scores to five and Weismann's to seven.

Made a *Chevalier de la Légion d'Honneur* on 27 March 1919, Jannekeyn competed in the 1924 Olympics in sabre fencing. Weismann, whose 131 missions included 40 bombardments and 20 aerial combats, was made a *Chevalier de la Légion d'Honneur* on 22 June 1919. After a hiatus Paillard joined the Lignes Farman airline and, in 1926, worked for the Société Bernard as a test pilot. He also planned to compete in the 1931 Schneider Trophy race, but whilst being operated on for appendicitis on 15 June that same year he succumbed to peritonitis.

World War 2 and the French defeat in June 1940 drove Br132's surviving ace team down very different paths. As commander of the Vichy French air force in the Levant, *Général de Division* Jannekeyn supervised a spirited defence against the British invasion of Lebanon and Syria in May-June 1941. After surrender and repatriation to France, he rose to the position of air force chief of staff from 19 April 1942 to 28 March 1943, and was regarded as a trustworthy ally by the Germans.

Dismissed from the air service in July 1940, Weismann returned to German-occupied Paris. Judging this an unhealthy environment for Jews like himself, he went underground to fight with distinction for the *Forces Français de l'Interieur* and, after Paris' liberation in August 1944, in the revived *Armée de l'Air* as an artillery spotter. Decorated with the *Grande Croix de la Légion d'Honneur*, the *Croix de Guerre 39-45* with two *palmes* and the American Bronze Star, Weismann remained in aviation after 1945, co-founding an air transport company. Jannekeyn, in contrast, was arrested as a Nazi collaborator on 4 May 1947, though his sentence was commuted on 27 January 1949.

In a final ironic twist, the Breguet crewmen's paths converged in their last years. Jannekeyn died in Paris on 3 November 1971, and was buried in the military cemetery at Montparnasse. Weismann also died in Paris, on 20 July 1973, and was buried near Antoine Paillard in the Bagneux cemetery.

Capt Didier Lecour-Grandmaison's aggressive handling of the Caudron R 4, combined with good gunners, redefined the role of twin-engined, three-seat reconnaissance aircraft (*Jon Guttman*)

Triplace Aces

If any unit approached acemaking as a team sport, it was R46. Formed on 23 March 1915 and attached to the *VIe Armée* in the Aisne sector, the unit had six Caudron G 3s and four G 4s on strength at the end of February 1916, by which time one pilot had been killed in an accident and three crewmen wounded in action. That relatively serene state of affairs changed on 13 March when Capt Didier Lecour-Grandmaison replaced Capt Joseph Legardeur as commander, and on 13 June, when C46 re-equipped with Caudron R 4s.

Born in Nantes on 18 May 1889, Lecour-Grandmaison was a devout Catholic and a 1907 Saint-Cyr graduate who had served in the *26e Régiment de Dragons* until dissatisfaction with the cavalry turned him to aviation. He earned his brevet on 15 May 1915 and served in C47 prior to his reassignment as CO of C46. Although dedicated to the long-range photographic missions usually assigned to his crews, Lecour-Grandmaison soon displayed a belligerent attitude toward enemy aircraft that crossed his path. When he encountered an LVG over the Forêt de Bry on 15 July 1916, he promptly attacked it. Lecour-Grandmaison's observer, Lt Jules César Campion, and his rear gunner, Sol Léon Vitalis, made short work of the aeroplane, with R46's first victory being credited to all three crewmen – in Vitalis' case, this was his second aerial success.

Cpl Léon Vitalis mans the rear cockpit of a Caudron R 4 of R46, which carried twin Lewis machine guns. Vitalis, who was credited with seven victories, survived the war (*Jon Guttman*)

Born in Lodève on 15 February 1890, Marie Gaston Fulerand Léon Vitalis had served in the *7e Régiment de Cuirassiers* until discharged for medical reasons that seem to have stood in the way of his becoming an aerial gunner until sheer persistence prevailed in January 1916. After gunnery training at Cazaux he was assigned to N67, with whom he and Sgt Robert de Marolles shared in downing a Fokker E III north of Hill 304 on 28 April. Soon afterward N67 replaced its last Nieuport two-seaters with single-seat scouts and Vitalis asked for a transfer to triplaces, getting his wish when R46 took him on.

R46's next success involved another crew, namely Sous-Lts Jean Loste and Pierre Barbou and Sol Louis Martin, who, upon crossing the lines near St Christ on 27 July, encountered five German aircraft, one of which was a twin-engined machine. In the ensuing combat Martin used up several ammunition drums and, when they ran out, fought on with a carbine until the twin-engined aeroplane went down at Estrées-en-Chaussée, killing Gfr Georg Scholz and Ltn Hans Seulen. The Caudron returned in a pitiable shape and had to be flown to Paris for replacement two days later.

This aerial skirmish had started two more future triplace aces on their way. Jean Augustin Paul Joseph Loste, born in Toulon on 2 September 1893, obtained his civil pilot's licence on 7 November 1913 and qualified as a seaplane pilot on 23 March 1914. After a stint in the infantry he entered aviation on 2 January 1915, got his military pilot's brevet on 19 April and was assigned to C56 nine days later. Wounded on 18 June, he was promoted to sergent on 19 July and commissioned as a sous-lieutenant on 17 April 1916. On 20 June he transferred to R46.

'With Loste, we had a machine gunner called Martin who fired admirably', Pierre Barbou recalled in a 1970 interview. 'A simple soldier mechanic who asked to fly'. The son of a customs agent, Louis Honoré Martin was born in Paris on 18 October 1896. The French military was not accepting anyone under 18 when war broke out, but Martin falsely claimed to be one year older than he was so that he could enter aviation as a mechanic, joining C56 as a Soldat 2e Classe in late 1915. On 11 August he became a first mechanic and was initially assigned to Adj André Delorme, before joining Sous-Lt Loste. Loste's *'mécano'* rejoined him in R46 on 18 July 1916, at which point Martin was reclassified as a gunner.

The early career of Sous-Lt Jean Loste paralleled that of Vitalis, and he too was credited with seven victories by war's end (*Jon Guttman*)

Two more Germans fell to R 4 crews on 22 August at the cost of Sgt Pierre Steuer, who was mortally wounded. On 6 September Capt Lecour-Grandmaison, Sous-Lt Pierre Arthur and MdL Vitalis drove down a Fokker at Brie. Two days later Loste, Barbou and Martin, in concert with a second R 4 crewed by Sgt Étienne Combret and Brigs Achille Rousseaux and Georges Cadot, battled six enemy aeroplanes and were jointly credited with one of them.

Combret's observer, Achille Justin Ernest Rousseaux was born in Dijon on 29 August 1889, the son of a railway employee. Completing a two-year hitch in the *15e Régiment de Chasseurs á Cheval* in 1910, he opened a butcher's shop in Paris, but rejoined his old regiment when war broke out. While on leave Rousseaux married Marcelle Frémaux on 15 February 1915. Transferred to aviation on 3 January 1916, he joined N23 on 14 April and was then posted to R46.

On 20 October Lecour-Grandmaison, with Sous-Lt Gaston Laboussière and MdL Vitalis, shared the downing of an LVG with fellow Caudron team Cpl Paul Rivière, Sous-Lt Eugène Barbier and Sgt Louis Girod. During a reconnaissance on 1 November Loste descended to an altitude of 150 metres, where his gunners, Capt Guy de Peytes de Montcabrier and Martin, sent an enemy aeroplane down in flames over its own hangar. That was not confirmed, but as the Caudron fought its way through a clutch of enemy fighters, its crew was credited with bringing down two of the pursuers. Anti-aircraft fire finally caused the bullet-riddled aeroplane to crash land in Allied lines, injuring Martin.

10 November saw Lecour-Grandmaison, Vitalis and Rousseaux bring down a Roland east of Barleux, and on the 16th Loste, Vitalis and Rousseaux downed an Albatros at Brie. On 23 November Adj Barbier, with Rousseaux and Adj Robert Mazeron, took on three Germans and downed an Aviatik. Between the enemy aeroplanes and anti-aircraft fire, the Caudron returned holed like a sieve, with Rousseaux wounded in the

Photographed in early 1917, this Caudron R 4 of R46 also served as the backdrop for a photo of Adj Achille Rousseaux, suggesting that he was probably part of its crew at some point during his career (*SHD B76-1144*)

arm. Loste, Barbou and Martin claimed a German aeroplane near Barleux on 27 December, and on 26 January the same team accounted for an Aviatik north of Bapaume. This, along with two more successes on 29 January 1917, brought R46's overall tally to a remarkable 22 for the loss of four men killed. The squadron was then withdrawn to replace its Caudrons with a somewhat improved triplace, the Letord 1A3.

In March 1917 Let46 was attached to the famous *Groupe de Combat* (GC) 12 *'Les Cigognes'*. Serving alongside the stork-marked Nieuports and SPADs of *escadrilles* N3, N26, N73 and N103, Lecour-Grandmaison and his Caudron crews had blurred the distinction between reconnaissance and fighter aircraft, much as the FE 2d had done in the RFC. When the *escadrille* resumed combat for Gen Nivelle's April 1917 Aisne offensive, however, it found deadlier opposition, which exacted a higher price for glory, awaiting it.

Let46 had its first encounter with the new *Jagdstaffeln* on 8 April when its three remaining R 4s were attacked by Albatros D IIIs of *Jasta* 19. Lt Marcel Bloch and Sgts Léonard Joussen and Alfred Boyé were credited with one Albatros over Aguilcourt. Claims by the team of Sgt Marcel Gendronneau, Lt René Wilmès and Adj Pierre de Cuypers and Cpls Maurice Damenez and Paul Rivière and MdL Célestin Théron were not confirmed. While some of its aeroplanes may have force landed, *Jasta* 19 suffered no casualties, while crediting a Caudron to Oblt Erich Hahn. That would have been Gendronneau's aeroplane, which limped in with Wilmès dead and de Cuypers wounded. Additionally, Théron was killed and Joussen wounded in the melee.

Deteriorating health led to Soldat 1e Classe Rousseaux's transfer from the army to the air service on January 1916. After gunnery training at Cazaux he went to N23, then R46 (*Jon Guttman*)

Capt Lecour-Grandmaison finally joined the ranks of his squadron's aces on 14 April when he, Vitalis and Rousseaux destroyed an Albatros in flames south of Craonne, killing Ltn Otto Weigel of *Jasta* 14. A second victory on the 17th was marred by Joussen being wounded for a second time. Gendronneau, with Asp Pierre Bruel and Cpl Georges Cadot at the guns, scored on the 26th, but on the 29th Letord N° 90 was lost, with all three crewmen, Lt Jules Campion, MdL Marcel Lamy and Cpl Bosquié, being killed. Its demise was credited to Ltn Walter Böning of *Jasta* 19.

The *escadrille*'s most jarring loss came on 10 May when Lecour-Grandmaison's Letord was beset by Albatros D Vs of *Jasta* 15 and shot down north of Berry-au-Bac by Ltn Heinrich Gontermann. Both Lecour-Grandmaison and Cpl Joseph Crozet perished, although the wounded rear gunner, Sgt Boyé, miraculously survived the Letord's crash-landing in Allied lines.

Shaken though Let46 was by the death of its CO, who was the unit's heart and soul, his Jewish successor, Lt Bloch, resolved to uphold Lecour-Grandmaison's aggressive legacy. In June the *escadrille* was detached from GC12 and reassigned to the *IIIe Armée*. By year-end its score stood at 28, although its tally of dead aircrew had risen somewhat dramatically to 15.

On 10 February 1918 Let46 reverted to its previous designation of R46 following the delivery of ten new Caudron R 11A3s – sleeker, more powerful, faster developments of the R 4, armed with as many as five machine guns each. With these machines it was attached to *Escadre de Combat* No 1, often escorting Breguet 14B2 bombers.

Adj Maurice Damenez, with Sous-Lt Paul Tison and Adj André Astoin, downed an enemy aeroplane on 18 April. They were in action again on 16 May when their aeroplane was attacked by ten Fokker Dr I triplanes. Together with another Caudron crew, and three intervening Sopwith Camels of No 209 Sqn RAF flown by Capt Stearne T Edwards and Lts Merril S Taylor and Wilfred R May, they drove Dr I 546/17 down in British lines near Corbie, where Ltn Hans Fedor Hübner of *Jasta* 4 was taken prisoner. Astoin had been wounded, however, and during yet another engagement on 21 May Tison was also hit, dying of his wounds the next day.

On 26 September Adj Damenez, Sgt Jules Jourde and Cpl Gustave Galotte downed an enemy fighter, bringing R46's final tally to 36 (more than a good many single-seat fighter *escadrilles* could claim) for the loss of 33 aircrew – 26 more were wounded – in combat. The unit produced five aces, namely Loste and Vitalis with seven victories each, Martin with six and Lecour-Grandmaison and Rousseaux with five.

Sgt Rousseaux, after being hospitalised on 12 September 1917 and subsequent brief service with N79, went to N88 on 5 October. On 2 December he was on a reconnaissance mission in one of two SPAD XIs when they encountered an enemy two-seater. As the French aeroplanes attacked they were joined by a SPAD VII that helped them send the German machine down in flames south of Ployart, killing Ltns Erich Pohl and Otto Heilmann of *Fl Abt (A)* 255s. Rousseaux shared his sixth victory with his pilot, Sgt Jean Vidal, and the other aircrew, Brig Jacques Wurtz and Cpl Eugène Cabot, as well as the scout pilot, Sous-Lt Raoul Lufbery of SPA124 'Lafayette', who within the hour would down another two-seater for his 16th, and final, confirmed victory.

Adj Rousseaux left SPA88 on 20 February 1918 and served as a gunnery instructor until 26 March 1919, when he was demobilised and returned to work at the Abbatoirs de la Villette in Paris. In 1928, however, he injured his hand while butchering a bull, and the subsequent amputation of his hand and, later, his arm were too late to stem the spread of gangrene that claimed his life on 23 October.

Americans attached to R46 in the summer of 1918. They are, from left to right, 2Lts Paul Penfield and 'Pop' Smith, Sgt Glenn N Sitterly and 2Lts Valentine J Burger, Alexander T Grier and Horace A Lake. Aside from Sitterly, who was a Lafayette Flying Corps pilot, the USAS personnel were all observers. Burger scored one victory with R46 on 11 August 1918 and three more in Salmson 2A2s with the 90th Aero Squadron. On 15 August Lake downed a German machine, but the *escadrille* lost two aeroplanes, the six crewmen killed including Penfield and another LFC volunteer, Soldat William J McKerness (*Valentine J Burger album via Jon Guttman*)

Made a *Chevalier de la Légion d'Honneur* on 29 December 1919, Léon Vitalis helped found the *Association Nationale des As* and on 14 July 1935 he was made a *Commandeur de la Légion d'Honneur*. He died at Lodève on 17 August 1941. Jean Loste rose to the grade of *Grand Officier de la Légion d'Honneur* before his death in Bordeaux on 26 July 1960.

Although plagued by ill health, Honoré Martin obtained his pilot's brevet, along with a promotion to *caporal*, on 12 April 1918. He joined SPA97 on 12 October, only to return to hospital ten days later. France's lowest ranking ace finally succumbed to his medical maladies on 27 January 1920.

A Caudron R 11 of R240 in the late summer of 1918. While R46 symbolised its three-seaters with a trident insignia, R240 marked its triplaces with a three-headed hydra (*David Méchin collection*)

Another triplace unit, R240, boasted at least one ace gunner. Alexandre Jean Marie Buisson was born on 17 September 1886 in Asnières-sur-Seine, the son of Jean Marie Buisson and Rumanian-born Katitza Lupesco. He enlisted in the army on 31 May 1905, serving in the *5e Régiment de Chasseurs d'Afrique* in Algeria and Morocco until 1908. Buisson was working an agronomy engineer in Paris when war broke out, and he joined the *8e Régiment de Hussards* before transferring to aviation on 3 June 1916. After training at Cazaux and Pau, MdL Buisson was assigned to F29.

On 12 October 1916 Buisson, with Sgt Marius Despert as his pilot, participated in the epic raid on the Mauser factory in Oberndorf that involved F29, F123, BM120 and 3 Naval Wing, Royal Naval Air Service, escorted by four Nieuport 17s of N124. Although the Allies suffered heavy losses overall, F29 got through relatively unscathed. Indeed, a Fokker that attacked Despert's Farman was shot down by Buisson for his first aerial victory.

Buisson subsequently served in Sop123 and C21. On 20 July 1918 the veteran was assigned to newly formed R240, and on 29 August, with Sgt Lucien Carteron as his pilot and Sgt A Gagne as front gunner, he was credited with an enemy fighter near Semide. On 1 October Buisson was promoted to adjudant, and the next day he was up front in Carteron's Caudron R 11, with Soldat E Raymond as rear gunner, when they despatched a Fokker in flames over Semide. Buisson's last two successes, shared with pilot Sgt J Dufour and the newly promoted Sgt Raymond, were described in his *Médaille Militaire* citation;

'On 3 November 1918, at the end of a protection mission, upon noticing an enemy convoy he descended along the German lines to strafe it. Attacked by a patrol of ten aeroplanes, he sustained a severe and unequal fight, permitting his pilot to disengage. He succeeded in downing two of his adversaries, one going down in flames and the other crashing to earth.'

Awarded the *Croix de Guerre*, Buisson returned to civilian endeavours post-war, but died in 1939.

Some French sources credit a second R240 gunner, Sgt André Coolen, with five victories, but his only documented successes were an enemy aeroplane on 22 July 1918, one in French lines seven days later, a two-seater on 29 August and a fourth shootdown on 4 November.

After claiming an enemy aeroplane shot down as a bombardier in F29 during the Oberndorf bombing raid of 12 October 1916, Adj Alexandre Buisson figured in four of R240's seven victories (*David Méchin collection*)

RFC, RNAS, RAF AND INDEPENDENT FORCE

Although the RFC used a variety of reconnaissance aeroplanes during the course of the war, its mainstay from the beginning was the Royal Aircraft Factory's Blériot Experimental BE 2. A stable and versatile machine, its shortcomings did not come fully to light until the Fokker Eindeckers made survivability in air-to-air combat a serious factor. Aside from its sluggish performance, the BE 2's placement of the observer up front amid a wilderness of cabane struts and cables, manning a Lewis gun stuck in one of two sockets on either side of the cockpit, truly rendered it 'Fokker fodder'. In spite of that, a handful of skilful – and lucky – BE crewmen were credited with the occasional victory before going on to better things, usually in fighter squadrons.

The British regarded their two-place pushers as 'reconnaissance fighters', with FB 5s, FE 2bs and FE 2ds expected to mix it with any opposition they encountered – until twin-gunned Albatros D IIs and D IIIs began

RE 8 crewmen of No 12 Sqn are briefed before a mission. In the course of corps observation, artillery spotting and troop support duties, two of the squadron's airmen, Lts Croye R Pithey and Hervey Rhodes, achieved double acedom with ten and eleven victories, respectively (*Colin Owers*)

running rings around them. Tractor-engined Bristol F 2B Fighters took over their role, especially long-range missions, admirably.

An in-flight photograph of an RE 8 of No 59 Sqn on a mission. For most of 1918 RFC/RAF unit markings were limited to a flight letter and individual numeral, as seen here (*RAF Museum*)

By 1917 the RFC was fielding two BE successors for frontline corps reconnaissance. The Royal Aircraft Factory RE 8 was essentially an improved BE 2e, retaining its redesigned single-bay wings with the upper of greater span than the lower, but at least the pilot was repositioned forward and the observer aft, with an immeasurably better field of defensive fire than his hapless predecessors. The same could be said of the Frederick Koolhoven-designed Armstrong-Whitworth FK 8. Two Victoria Crosses were earned in the robust FK 8s, by 2Lt Alan Arnett McLeod of No 2 Sqn on 27 March 1918 and Capt Ferdinand Maurice Felix West of No 8 Sqn on 12 August 1918. It was in the RE 8, however, that one remarkable duo achieved the implausible status of double acedom.

Croye Rothes Pithey was born in Rothesdale, Scheedersnek, Natal, South Africa, on 19 August 1895. Fluent in Zulu, he worked as an accounts clerk in Johannesburg until May 1917, when he joined the RFC. Pithey initially served as a pilot in No 52 Sqn, but illness cut short his time there. Upon recovery he joined No 12 Sqn on 17 April 1918, by which time the RFC had been incorporated into the Royal Air Force and the Germans had launched their last great offensive in the West. Pithey began flying corps missions with Lt Hervey Rhodes.

Born on 12 August 1895 and hailing from Saddleworth, West Riding, Yorkshire, Rhodes had worked in the woollen industry since he was 12, but had also studied at St Marys School, Greenfield, and Huddersfield Technical College. When war broke out he served in the King's Own Royal Lancashire Regiment and the Yorkshire Regiment, prior to assignment to the Signals Platoon of 7th Battalion, King's Own Royal Lancashire Regiment. From there he transitioned into the RFC as an observer, joining No 12 Sqn in March 1918.

Pithey and Rhodes first bared their collective fangs on 7 May when they spotted a kite balloon on the ground behind German lines. Pithey descended to 1700 ft, at which point Rhodes fired three ten-round bursts and the balloon went up in flames. The next day Rhodes, with 2Lt N Garland as his pilot, drove an enemy aeroplane down out of control (OOC). Reunited in RE 8 B7715, Pithey and Rhodes were flying a morning patrol on 4 June when another balloon emerged from a cloud in front of them. Pithey simply fired his Vickers gun and it burst into flamc. Three days later they found themselves on the receiving end when they spotted nine Pfalz D IIIas circling above, two of which dived at them from behind. Coolly waiting as the range closed, Rhodes fired several bursts and saw one Pfalz continue its dive, apparently OOC. A second pair then attacked, and after firing 120 rounds Rhodes sent another Pfalz spinning down. When a third duo came down, Rhodes fired at the leader and saw it off with a shattered tail.

Pithey was slightly wounded by ground fire on 24 July, and while recuperating he and Rhodes were gazetted for the Distinguished Flying Cross (DFC) on 3 August. During a contact patrol on 21 August they were successively attacked by four Fokker D VIIs. Rhodes drove one down OOC, but as they neared the lines the last Fokker struck their fuel tank. With petrol leaking in their faces and fire an imminent danger, Rhodes clambered out on the wing to plug the hole with his glove. A frontline observer must have seen this unusual sight from the ground and reported it to No 12 Sqn, for upon their landing the unit CO, Maj T Q Back, demanded to know why Pithey and Rhodes were performing wing-walking aerobatics. A quick explanation of their predicament turned his criticism to praise.

During a contact patrol over Boyelles, Pithey and Rhodes encountered an LVG, which both men fired upon and reported shooting down in flames. Flying RE 8 F6097 over St Leger on 28 August, they spotted a DFW C V conducting a frontline reconnaissance of its own. Thrice they attacked the DFW, which retired, only to turn and chase them when they in turn headed westward for home. Finally, Pithey quickly reversed direction and dived after the enemy aeroplane, closing to 150 yards for Rhodes to get in a burst with his twin Lewis guns. Moments later the DFW stalled and crashed.

On 30 August Pithey and Rhodes assailed another enemy two-seater, but without result, then encountered seven Fokker D VIIs near Bullecourt. Firing at each target that presented itself, Rhodes saw one Fokker explode in flames and spin down. Another RE 8 subsequently turned up and some of the Fokkers went after it, only to be driven off by Pithey and Rhodes. 'We had numerous forays tempting would-be executioners to try their arm with us and ensure their own destruction', Rhodes later stated. 'Although we were very slow, we had a perfect understanding, and once we got them in the position we wanted them it was easy'.

While on a contact patrol on 1 September Pithey and Rhodes drove off a similarly engaged German two-seater, only to see it return with six fighters. Although shot about, the duo drove off their attackers and completed their mission. On the 3rd they attacked an LVG, which Rhodes sent down to crash near Lagnicourt, bringing his personal tally to 11 and Pithey's to ten.

On 16 September No 12 Sqn moved up from Sombrin to Vrau Vraucourt. Rhodes was due for home leave with the prospect of pilot training on the 26th, but he asked for one more day of flying prior to Pithey's imminent release. When granting this, the VI Corps commander, Lt Gen James A L Haldane, added a personal request for the redoubtable pair's support in a British offensive against the Hindenburg Line scheduled for the next morning.

The first assault over the St Quentin canal commenced at 0530 hrs on 27 September and Pithey and Rhodes duly completed their mission, with the latter laughing off a bad premonition he had had the night before. He was keen for one more sortie. 'An aeroplane came in that had only been up for half-an-hour as the pilot had suffered an arm wound', Pithey recalled. 'We rushed over to see if they had done their patrol and, as they hadn't, up we went'. At the dry Canal du Nord they spotted a German battery being manhandled onto the road for horsedrawn evacuation. Pithey dived down to strafe it, and during the aeroplane's second pass return fire struck him in the arm and Rhodes in the leg and buttock. Pithey returned to Vrau Vraucourt, where Rhodes, collapsed in an observer's pit awash in blood, was extricated only with great difficulty.

On 3 December the RE 8 team received bars to their DFCs. Rhodes, who had been gravely wounded, did not recover from his injuries sufficiently to be released from hospital until 1921, by which time his intrepid partner was dead. Serving successively in Nos 106 and 105 Sqns in 1919, Pithey was in No 2 Sqn on 21 December 1920 when he departed Shotwick, in Chester, leading a ferry flight of three Bristol Fighters to Baldonnell, in Ireland. He was last seen aloft between Denbigh and Rhyl, in Wales, but crashed shortly thereafter. His remains were buried in Hollybrooke Memorial Cemetery in Southampton.

Returning to wool manufacturing, Rhodes acquired a mill at Delph, near Oldham. In World War 2 he commanded the Local Defence Volunteers, later renamed the Home Guard, and also entered politics as a Labour candidate, becoming a Member of Parliament for Ashton-under-Lyne from 1945 to 1964, and serving as Parliamentary Secretary to the Board of Trade in 1950-51 and in 1964-67. In 1968 Rhodes was made Lord Lieutenant of Lancashire, having become a baron four years earlier. Serving on the Privy Council from 1969, Lord Rhodes spent his last years in Oldham, Lancashire, until his death on 11 September 1987.

Another exceptional RE 8 pilot, Douglas Hugh Moffatt Carbery was born in Ambala, India, on 26 March 1894, but following his father's death in 1913 he journeyed to England. After graduating from King's School in Bruton, Somerset, he entered the Royal Military Academy, and in August 1914 he served in the 96th Battery of the Royal Heavy Artillery. Wounded in May and July 1915, Carbery transferred to the RFC on 20 April 1916, and after flight training joined No 52 Sqn.

While flying new RE 8 A81 on 25 January 1917, Lt Carbery and 2Lt H A D MacKay brought a two-seater down in Allied lines near Morlancourt – the crew, Ltn d Rs Ewald Erdmann and Günther Kallenbach of Royal Württemberg *Fl Abt (A)* 216, died of their wounds. On 14 February Carbery was in BE 2e 6755 when his observer, 2Lt M A S Vaile, drove an Albatros D III down OOC. Sharing the credit, Carbery was gazetted for the Military Cross (MC) on 26 March.

During a second tour of duty Carbery led an RE 8 flight in No 9 Sqn and served as an instructor in No 15 (Training) Sqn, before returning to France with No 59 Sqn in August 1918. On the 30th of that same month he and his observer, Lt J B V Clements, drove a Fokker D VII down OOC over Beugnâtre. Nine days later they destroyed a Halberstadt two-seater. On 24 September Carbery and Lt R N Ireland destroyed a Halberstadt near Gonnelieu and on the 28th Carbery and Clements downed yet another one at La Vacquerie. With six victories to his name Capt Carbery received the DFC on 3 December.

Flying with No 31 Sqn in India from March 1919, Carbery was awarded a bar to his DFC on 12 July 1920 for service in Afghanistan. Later that same year he rejoined the Royal Artillery in India, and in World

Besides scoring six victories, Capt Douglas H M Carbery excelled at close support with No 59 Sqn. For example, between 1450 hrs and 1800 hrs on 25 August 1918 he and 2Lt J B V Clements carried out four artillery shoots and attacked three ground targets. Then on 28 September they attacked a German field piece with four 25-lb Cooper bombs, disabling the limber and driving off the crew. British troops who captured the gun presented it to the RAF as a trophy (*Norman Franks*)

War 2 he served in West Africa and Burma. Retiring as a brigadier in 1946, Carbery resided in Lanner, Cornwall, until his death in April 1959.

Sopwith Strutters

The BE was not the only British reconnaissance aeroplane to suffer from rapid advances in aerial warfare. While the RFC was developing pushers in response to the 'Fokker scourge', Thomas O M Sopwith and his chief engineer, Herbert Smith, unveiled a different approach for the Royal Naval Air Service (RNAS) on 12 December 1915. A single-bay biplane powered by a 110 hp Clerget 9Z engine and named for its W-shaped cabane strut arrangement, the Sopwith '1½ Strutter' was the first British tractor warplane to mount a synchronised forward-firing Vickers machine gun. There was also a Lewis gun on a flexible ring mounting, designed by the RNAS's WO Frederick W Scarff, for the observer.

Built as both a two-seat 'reconnaissance fighter' and in single-seat form to accommodate a bomb load, the 1½ Strutter would later be adopted by the RFC and license-produced in even greater numbers by the French. In the summer of 1916 the RNAS was using its Sopwiths either as bombers or as their escorts. The RFC sent No 70 Sqn to the front equipped with two-seaters in June 1916, followed by No 45 Sqn in October. By September, however, the Fokkers had been replaced by a newer, more potent 'scourge' in the form of the Albatros D II, and when No 43 Sqn's 1½ Strutters entered combat in January 1917 the Albatros D III had made its debut.

Outclassed in performance, the Sopwith two-seater's usefulness in fighter patrols waned and its aircrews soon had their hands full performing the reconnaissance role. Even so, a handful of individuals achieved ace status, all with No 45 Sqn at Ste-Marie-Cappel.

The highest-scoring 1½ Strutter pilot with 13 victories, Geoffrey Hornblower Cock was born in Shrewsbury, Shropshire, on 7 January 1896 and joined the 28th London Regiment, the Artists' Rifles Officers Training Corps, in December 1915. In June 1916 Cock switched to the RFC, earning his wings in No 25 Reserve Sqn in September and joining No 45 Sqn the following month (*Norman Franks*)

On 7 February 1917 Lt James Dacres Belgrave and Sub-Lt John Thompson, an attached observer from the Royal Naval Volunteer Reserve, drove an Albatros down OOC over Menin, and on 18 March Belgrave and 2Lt Francis G Truscott destroyed a two-seater in flames northeast of Ploegsteert Wood. On 6 April a patrol had just completed its photography when it was attacked by Albatros D IIIs of *Jasta* 30, losing one aeroplane to Oblt Hans Bethge and two to Ltn Joachim von Bertrab. The latter then attacked A1075 flown by 2Lt Geoffrey Hornblower Cock, who reported that after his observer, 2Lt John Thompson Guy Murison (a 28-year-old former pharmaceutical chemist from Muswell Hill, London), fired 50 rounds into the aeroplane from a distance of just 30 yards. 'He fell to pieces and went down on top of our two wrecked machines'. Cock was credited with this D III and a second adversary that No 45 Sqn claimed in the fight, although von Bertrab himself was unharmed. Cock also noted, with underlining for emphasis, that 'Every hostile machine <u>completely outmanoeuvred</u> us, and they were capable of beating us in a climb, when turning and in outright speed'.

Belgrave, with 2Lt Charles G Stewart as his observer, claimed an Albatros D III OOC on 5 May, followed by another on the 7th, when Cock and Murison were also credited with a Siemens-Schuckert D I and 2Lts C W Carleton and John Arthur Vessey from Rochdale, Lancashire, with an Albatros D III OOC near Lille. The squadron suffered two losses in a scrap with *Jasta* 28 on the 9th, but Cock and Murison were credited with an opponent in flames and shared a second victory with 2Lt William A Wright and Lt Edward T Caulfield-Kelly from County Galway, Ireland. Another 'flamer' west of Menin was credited to 2Lt James Johnstone and 2AM T M Harries in Sopwith A963.

Born in Menstrie, Scotland, in October 1888, 2AM Thomas Montagu Harries proved to be one of No 45 Sqn's deadliest gunners. On 12 May he and Johnstone brought an Albatros C V of *Fl Abt* (*Lichtbild*) 18 down east of Armentières, Ltn Rolf Dyck dying of wounds and Ltn Walther Mohr being taken prisoner. An Albatros D III was also credited that day to Canadian 2Lts R S Watt and George Walker Blaiklock.

During another major encounter eight days later Cock and 2Lt Allan S Carey downed an Albatros D III OOC near Lille while Sgt Ernest A Cook and 2Lt Blaiklock claimed an Albatros and a Halberstadt. Capt Christopher H Jenkins was mortally wounded, however, and Cock, besides receiving the MC, replaced him as 'B' Flight leader.

During an encounter over Zonnebeke on 24 May Wright and Caulfield-Kelly were credited with an Albatros in flames, and they shared another one OOC with Belgrave and Stewart and Lts Philip T Newling and W E Holland. The next day Capt Gordon Mountford and 2Lt Vessey downed two Albatros D IIIs OOC over Dadizeele, but 2Lts James Johnstone and Thomas S Millar were brought down by Vfw Karolus Bärenfänger of *Jasta* 28 and captured.

On 27 May Cock and Caulfield-Kelly drove a D III down OOC over Menin, as did Mountford and Vessey and Belgrave and 2Lt G A H Davis over Roulers, but 'C' Flight lost its leader, Capt Lawrence W McArthur, and 2Lt Carey, killed by Offz Stv Max Müller of *Jasta* 28. In a fight over Menin on the 28th Caulfield-Kelly was wounded, but not before he and Wright despatched an Albatros in flames, while Cock and 2Lt Wilfred G Corner downed a second.

The teams of Mountford and Vessey and 2Lt Robert M Findlay and Lt Blaiklock were each credited with an Albatros D V OOC over Comines on 31 May, Vessey's being his fifth success. The next day Belgrave, having scored six victories and been awarded the MC, was withdrawn for home defence duty with No 61 Sqn. Capt Belgrave returned to France in April 1918 as a flight commander in No 60 Sqn and scored 12 more victories in SE 5as before he was killed on 13 June, either by return fire from the two-seater he had just jointly shot down or ground fire.

On 3 June 2Lt Watt and Cpl Harries destroyed a D III southeast of Quesnoy. Two days later 22-year-old Glaswegian 2Lt Matthew Brown Frew was credited with an

James Dacres Belgrave was born in Kensington, London, on 26 September 1896, and he served in the Oxford and Bucks Light Infantry from December 1914 until wounded on November 1915. Joining the RFC, he began pilot training in July 1916, and on 30 November Belgrave was posted to No 45 Sqn. While serving with this unit he was credited with six victories flying Sopwith 1½ Strutters, followed by 12 in SE 5as with No 60 Sqn (*Norman Franks*)

Matthew Brown Frew, born in Glasgow on 7 April 1895, served in the Highland Light Infantry, transferring to the RFC in August 1916 and joining No 45 Sqn on 28 April 1917. After five victories in 1½ Strutters he subsequently became the squadron's leading ace in Camels, his final tally reaching 23 (*Norman Franks*)

2Lt Victor Rodney Stokes White earned an MC with the 3rd Reserve Battalion of the Stafford Regiment, Special Reserve before becoming an observer in No 45 Sqn. After sharing in an Albatros D III with Capt Cock on 13 July 1917, he transferred on 1 September to No 20 Sqn, with whom he added five more to his tally in Bristol F 2Bs and received a Bar to his MC on 6 April 1918 (*Norman Franks*)

Albatros D III OOC, while his observer, 2Lt M J Dalton, got one in flames. Three aeroplanes were lost, however, to Ltns Karl Allmenröder, Otto Brauneck and Alfred Niederhoff of *Jasta* 11, and Ltn Richard Runge of *Jasta* 18 forced a fourth Sopwith down in British lines, with Newling and Corner wounded.

Tragedy struck on 12 June when Mountford and Vessey, returning from a sortie, collided with 2Lt Watt and 2AM Walter Pocock, who were just taking off to escort a six-aeroplane reconnaissance mission. All four men died.

Re-equipped with 1½ Strutters powered by 130 hp 9B Clergets, No 45 Sqn found that the extra 20 hp made scant difference during a fight over Comines on 16 June. Five Albatros scouts were claimed OOC, including one each to the teams of Cock and Murison, Frew and Dalton and Capt Findlay and Lt Blaiklock, but two more aeroplanes were lost to Oblt Eduard Dostler of *Jasta* 6 and Vfw Kurt Wüsthoff of *Jasta* 4.

Aerial activity intensified in July as the Allies prepared to launch a new offensive in Flanders. Cock and Lt C T R Ward claimed an Albatros northeast of Comines on the 6th and one over Wervicq on the 7th, while on the latter date Lts E F Crossland and Blaiklock claimed another and Cpl Harries, with Sgt R E Yeomans as his pilot, downed an Albatros D V in flames and claimed two others OOC. Again the squadron lost two aeroplanes, to Ltn Hans Klein of *Jasta* 4 and Vfw Josef Lautenschlager of *Jasta* 11.

On 13 July Cock and 2Lt Victor R S White downed an Albatros east of Polygon Wood, and three days later 2Lts Frew and G A Brooke destroyed a D III in flames over Polygon Wood. Cpl Harries left the squadron on 16 July. Later commissioned and becoming a pilot, Harries added five more victories to his tally flying SE 5as with No 24 Sqn in the summer of 1918. Gazetted for the DFC on 20 February 1919, he left the RAF on 20 September and spent his later years in Warminster, Wiltshire.

In yet another run-in with *Jasta* 11 on 22 July No 45 Sqn claimed three opponents, including one OOC by Crossland and Blaiklock (this was the latter's sixth victory). Two more aeroplanes were lost, however, 2Lts Robert H Deakin and Reginald Hayes falling in flames to Ltn Niederhoff. The other, Cock's B2576, was hit by the German leader, Oblt Wilhelm Reinhard, after the observer, Lt Maurice Moore, suffered a gun jam. Determined to put up a fight, Cock, using his forward Vickers, managed to set an assailant afire before crashing into a shell hole near Warneton, where he and Moore were captured.

The last of No 45 Sqn's original complement of pilots who had flown to France in October 1916, Cock had completed 97 sorties and claimed 19 victories (nine using his front gun), of which 13 were confirmed, making him the highest-scoring 'Strutter' pilot. After an abortive escape attempt, he was finally released in December 1918 and remained with the RAF, retiring with the rank of group captain in 1943. Cock died in Belford, Northumberland, on 16 February 1980.

Frew and Brooke destroyed a D III on 28 July and sent another down OOC east of Comines on 10 August. 'Bunty' Frew then flew Camels over France and Italy, becoming No 45 Sqn's leading ace with a total of 23. Retiring from the RAF as an air vice marshal, Sir Matthew Frew died in Pretoria, South Africa, on 28 May 1974.

Withdrawn on 1 September, Canadian George Blaiklock instructed in photography and gunnery upon returning home, but his request for pilot training was denied. Resigning his RAF commision on 31 March 1919, he died in Montreal on 13 July 1977, aged 85.

John Murison instructed at No 199(N) Training Squadron and became a pilot in 1918. He died in March 1936.

— RNAS, RFC AND RAF BOMBER TEAMS —

Aside from the occasional tactical raid, Britain's first significant bombing campaign was mounted by the RNAS. On 16 June 1916 3 Naval Wing, equipped with Sopwith 1½ Strutters, arrived at Luxeuil-les-Bains to join the French bombing of Germany's industrial Saar region.

In January 1917 Gen Sir Douglas Haig (commander of the BEF) and Maj Gen Hugh M Trenchard (commander of the RFC) decided that in light of heavy losses suffered by the RFC in recent months, 3 Naval Wing's bombing constituted an inadequately productive diversion of men and machines from more vital air operations. Therefore, they began transferring pilots from the wing to newly formed fighter squadrons, starting that month with Canadians Ray Collishaw, Joseph S T Fall, James A Glen, John J Malone and Arthur T Whealy. They would be followed by William Melville Alexander, George B Anderson, Frederick C Armstrong, Alfred W Carter, William H Chisam, Desmond F Fitzgibbon, John A Page, Ellis V Reid and John E Sharman. All of them would distinguish themselves in fighters, along with Englishman Flt Ldr Christopher Draper (as recounted in *Osprey Aircraft of the Ace 97 – Naval Aces of World War 1, Part 1*). After its 18th raid, on Breiburg on 14 April, the last of 3 Naval Wing's airmen were withdrawn and its Sopwiths bequeathed to the French.

Both the RNAS and the RFC mounted tactical bombing raids along the front from Flanders to the Somme throughout 1917. German *Jagdstaffeln* regularly opposed them, often leading to heavy losses and a number of British aircrews being credited with victories in turn. Actual German losses tended to be a fraction of those claimed, not least because any of their badly hit fighters generally came down in their lines, to be repaired and returned to service. In contrast, returning British bombers had to fight the prevailing westerly winds, and if they were brought down it was usually in enemy territory.

The most active RNAS units over Flanders in 1917 were 2 and 5 Naval Squadrons, whose Sopwiths gave way later in the year to more powerful and robust Airco DH 4s. On 1 April 1918 they were amalgamated into the RAF as Nos 202 and 205 Sqns, respectively, and several aircrewmen who were already aces added to their scores in that capacity, while others completed their scoring or became aces under RAF auspices. The latter included 2Lt Robert Chalmers from Glasgow and Lt Cyril Justin Heywood from Hagley, Stourbridge, both of whom scored six victories with No 205 Sqn,

Thomas Frederick Le Mesurier was born in Merton Park, Surrey, on 16 February 1897. Joining the RNAS on 23 July 1915, he obtained his aero certificate on 17 March 1916. Posted to 5 Naval Squadron in February 1917, he scored seven victories in DH 4s (six of them with Gunlayer H S Jackson as his observer). Later serving with 11 Naval Squadron, which became No 211 Sqn in the RAF from 1 April 1918, he and 2Lt R Lardner were killed on 26 May 1918 when their DH 9 D1693 broke up over Pervyse, probably due to flak damage. By then Le Mesurier had received the DSC and two Bars (*Norman Franks*)

Born in Weston-super-Mare, Somerset, on 3 January 1889, Charles Philip Oldfield Bartlett flew 101 bombing sorties in Sopwith 1½ Strutters and DH 4s with 5 Naval Squadron and its later RAF incarnation, No 205 Sqn. He was credited with eight victories, awarded the DSC and Bar and wrote a memoir, *Bomber Pilot*, before his death at the age of 97 (*Norman Franks*)

A Dubliner born on 24 January 1897, Eric Bourne Coulter Betts had been a signalman in the Royal Navy Volunteer Reserve before becoming an observer with 1 Naval Wing. He downed an Albatros D II OOC on 1 February 1917 in a Sopwith 1½ Strutter with 2 Naval Squadron, and after the unit became No 202 Sqn Capt Betts, with Lt Noel Keeble as his pilot, raised his tally to five. These successes earned him the DFC, while Keeble was awarded the DSO, DFC and Bar. Betts went on to become an acting air vice-marshal in World War 2, and later a Commander in the Order of the British Empire (CBE). He died on 30 October 1971 (*Norman Franks*)

as well as pilots Capt William Grossart from Dumfries, Scotland, and Lt William Henry Clarke from Harrogate, Yorkshire, as well as bombardier 2Lt Charles Myers Wickham from Halifax, Yorkshire, all three of whom were credited with five victories each. Sharing in Chalmers' six was his bombardier, 2Lt Stanley Herbert Hamblin from Newbury, Berkshire.

In No 202 Sqn, Lt Lionel Arthur Ashfield from Bury St Edmunds, Suffolk, was awarded the DFC for logging 62 sorties, 17 combats and five victories. On 27 June 1918 Ashfield and his observer, Lt N H Jenkins, were wounded, their 'demise' (Ashfield actually brought DH 4 A7868 home) almost certainly being credited to Flgmstr Hans Bossler of *Marine Feld Jasta* II. On 16 July, however, Ashfield, again in A7868, and his bombardier, Lt M H English, were killed near Ostende by Flgmstr Hans Goerth of MFJ III.

Of the many other ex-RNAS bomber units, only No 206 Sqn produced aces. Prominent among them was 19-year-old Capt Leslie Reginald Warren from Leamington Spa, who, in DH 9 B7596, was credited with eight victories, including a Pfalz D IIIa in flames on 1 July, three downed on 29 July and another two on 1 August. All six of those successes were shared with Lt Leo Arthur Christian, a former horse breeder from British Columbia who was not tall enough to be a pilot, but whose score as an observer totalled nine.

Squadronmate and fellow ace Rupert Norman Gould Atkinson was born to a merchant in Shanghai, China, on 17 July 1896. Educated at Marlborough, he forsook further schooling at Cambridge for a military career with the Middlesex Regiment and the West African Regiment in Cameroon, until invalided home in April 1916. Obtaining an Aero Club certificate on 28 September, Atkinson flew FK 8s with No 10 Sqn before switching to DH 9s in No 98 Sqn, in which he and Lt E A Shaw downed a Fokker Dr I and a Pfalz D IIIa in flames northwest of Roulers on 19 May 1918. Withdrawn for a rest in June, he returned as a flight leader in No 206 Sqn. With 2Lt Walter T Ganter as his bombardier, Atkinson was credited with a D VII on 30 August, a balloon on 4 September and another D VII shared with 2Lt John B Blamford on 14 October. With more than 1000 hours of combat flying and five victories in his log Atkinson was awarded the DFC and Bar and the Belgian *Croix de Guerre*. Although he survived the war, Atkinson became a fatality of the influenza epidemic on 7 March 1919.

Born in Sheffield on 31 March 1892, Euan Dickson worked as an engineer in New Zealand from 1912 to 1914, when he returned to England and joined the RNAS on 30 July 1916. Posted to fly fighters with 10 Naval Squadron on 31 March 1917, he was involved in a series of accidents that led to his transfer to DH 4-equipped 'Naval 5'. Dickson scored seven victories with that unit, and another seven after its re-designation as No 205 Sqn. He had completed 180 bombing sorties by August 1918. After a distinguished career as a flier and engineer in New Zealand, Dickson died in Auckland on 10 March 1980 (*Norman Franks*)

Of the multitude of RFC pilots and bombardiers who – not unlike their World War 2 descendants – were credited with multiple successes, a number stand out for additional aspects of their careers. One such individual was Percy Henry O'Lieff, born in Banbury, Oxon, on 8 May 1895 and initially seeing action as an observer with No 1 Sqn in Morane-Saulniers. On 8 September 1916, with 2Lt T M B Newton as his pilot, he drove down a Fokker E III that was not confirmed. On 27 November he and his pilot, the famous prewar dancer 2Lt Vernon W Castle, were credited with a two-seater over Vlamertinghe.

Starting out as an observer in No 20 Sqn with the rank of 2nd Air Mechanic, David Arthur Stewart downed two German scouts in August 1916, then became a pilot flying DH 4s with No 18 Sqn in the autumn of 1917. By 17 June 1918 Capt Stewart had claimed 16 victories and been awarded the DFC, MC and Bar. His first was an Albatros D V OOC on 6 January 1918 whilst flying with 20-year-old 2Lt Harry William Mackintosh MacKay from Aberdeen, Scotland. The two downed another four fighters over Port-à-Vendin on 6 March, but DH 4 A7797's controls were shot away during the course of the action and Stewart had to crash land in Allied lines. Although he emerged from the action unhurt, MacKay succumbed to his wounds a short while later (*Norman Franks*)

Subsequently serving as an air mechanic, O'Lieff applied for flight training and obtained a Royal Aero Club Certificate on 28 April 1917, as well as a commission. Returning to the front with No 55 Sqn, he was flying DH 4 A7592 when he and Cpl A Walters downed an Albatros D V in flames near Courtrai on 3 October 1917, and on 24 March 1918 when he and 2Lt S R Wells were credited with an Albatros destroyed and two OOC near Mannheim. O'Lieff's luck ran out on 5 April when he came down in Luxembourg and was taken prisoner. Little more is known of O'Lieff after he renewed his flying licence on 24 May 1939.

A different sort of mid-war career change befell Arthur Thomas Drinkwater, born on 3 February 1894 and hailing from Queenscliff, Victoria, Australia. Joining the RFC in November 1916 and commissioned on 19 March 1917, he flew DH 4s in No 57 Sqn. Drinkwater's bombardier from July onward, 21-year-old Lt Frank Tremar Silby Menendez from Midford, Bath, was the nephew of Sir M R Menendez. Educated at Wycliffe School and Cambridge, Menendez left school in March 1915 to join the 11th Yorks and Lancs Regiment, switching to the Gloucester Regiment in September of that same year and to the RFC in May 1917.

Drinkwater and Menendez downed an Albatros D V OOC over Courtrai on 18 August and another over the Houthulst Forest two days later. They destroyed an Albatros and sent another down OOC near Dadizeele on 21 September, and scored a double OOC southeast of Houthulst on 12 November. Awarded the MC on 27 October, Menendez returned to England in January 1918, but was injured in a flying accident on 1 August.

When Drinkwater returned from leave later that same month, it was as the leader of an SE 5a flight in No 40 Sqn, raising his total to nine as of 9 October and being gazetted for the DFC on 3 June 1919. Two days later his former observer, Menendez, resigned his commission due to ill health. Drinkwater died in Queenland in 1972, while Menendez, a retired civil servant, died in Eastbourne on 27 February 1973, aged 77.

Ace Killers of Fifty Seven

While their scores may have been exaggerated in the fog of war, every now and then the bomber crews drew real blood – and sometimes significant blood. Laurence Minot was one such individual, achieving his moment of glory against the 'Red Baron's' 'Flying Circus'.

Born on 21 July 1896, Minot gained Royal Aero Club Certificate 1409 on 8 July 1915, subsequently flying reconnaissance missions in Nos 16 and 7 Sqns. After rest leave he was posted to No 57 Sqn as a supernumerary flight leader in 1917, but circumstances soon altered his status.

Born in Upper Norwood, southeast London, Lt Laurence Minot went from supernumerary to flight leader in No 57 Sqn. His six victories included three on 7 July 1917, one of which turned out to be Oblt Albert Dossenbach, CO of *Jasta* 10 of *Jagdgeschwader* I. On 28 July, however, Minot had one encounter too many with the 'Red Baron's' 'Flying Circus' (*Norman Franks*)

Howard Redmayne Harker was born in Prestwich on 12 May 1891 and, after graduating with first class honours from Manchester University, he worked at the Royal Aircraft Factory's experimental department from February 1913. In April 1916 he joined the RFC and flew FE 2bs and DH 4s with No 57 Sqn, downing five German fighters between 24 March and 21 August 1917. Returning to the Home Establishment on 31 August, Harker served as acting commander of No 31 Training Squadron and died amid the influenza epidemic on 27 February 1919 (*Norman Franks*)

A farmer born at Petersfield on 26 October 1898, George William Francis Darvill gained his flying certificate at Hendon on 13 July 1917. He was assigned to No 9 Sqn in October, but on 13 January 1918 he went to No 18 Sqn. Flying DH 4s, he scored eight victories between 10 May and 12 August, for which he received the MC, the DFC and, on 18 August, appointment to flight leader. On 8 July, when his bombardier, 26-year-old Lt William Miller from Newcastle-on-Tyne, suffered a gun jam, Darville turned on three Fokker D VIIs and sent one down to crash. On 4 September the duo destroyed two D VIIs of *Jasta* 36, killing Ltn Kurt Waldhelm and mortally wounding Uffz Reinhold Neumann, for Darvill's ninth and Miller's sixth victory. Two days later Miller was wounded but Capt Darvill force landed their DH 4, A7815, in Allied lines. Rejoining the RAF in World War 2, Darvill died in Christchurch, Hampshire, in September 1950 (*Norman Franks*)

Born the son of a barrister in South Kensington, London, 27-year-old Capt Norman George McNaughton had flown FE 2bs with No 20 Sqn before being wounded in the leg. Returning to the front with No 57 Sqn, he and his observers were credited with five enemy aeroplanes, including two OOC on 4 March 1917 and another two on 29 April, for which McNaughton received the MC and command of 'B' Flight. In June the squadron replaced its FE 2bs with DH 4s, and on the morning of 24 June McNaughton and Lt Angus Hughes Mearns, in A7473, led a second DH 4 on a reconnaissance mission over Beceleaere with an escort of eight Sopwith Triplanes from 10 Naval Squadron led by Flt Lt Raymond Collishaw.

The naval pilots reported being attacked from above by at least 12 red Albatros D Vs, and although Collishaw claimed one of them, several of his men suffered gun jams and one of them, Flt Lt John E Sharman, saw some Germans get through to shoot down one of the DHs. McNaughton and Mearns crashed into a German hangar and their aeroplane exploded. Their remains were never recovered. They were credited to the leader of *Jagdgeschwader* I, Rittm Manfred *Freiherr* von Richthofen, as his 55th victory.

With McNaughton's death Minot was given command of 'B' Flight and assigned DH 4 A7487, with Lt Arthur Frederick Britton, a former soldier in the Machine Gun Corps from Streatham, south London, as his observer. On 3 July four of No 57 Sqn's DH 4s had another run-in with the 'Baron's' 'Circus' over Frezenburg, but with a different outcome – Minot and Britton were credited with one Albatros OOC and another in flames near Zonnebeke. The latter turned out to be Ltn Albert Dossenbach, an *Orden Pour le Mérite* recipient who had just taken command of *Jasta* 10 of JG I on 21 June and who had burned a balloon on the 27th for his 15th victory, before Minot and Britton killed him.

In a brief trade of observers, Minot and 1AM Goffe downed an Albatros D V OOC northeast of Ypres on 7 July, while Lt A D Pryor and Britton claimed another. Minot and Britton were reunited in DH 4 B3963 on 27 July, when they drove three Albatros D Vs down OOC over Houthulst. Britton was wounded, however, and the next day Minot flew A7540 with 2Lt Sidney J Leete as his observer on a bombing mission that had yet another encounter with a 'Circus' *Staffel*, *Jasta* 6. Minot and Leete were shot down and killed over Oostroosebeke, probably by Ltn Hans Adam.

Returning to action, Britton was engaged in a photo-reconnaissance mission on 20 August when his and the accompanying DH 4 were attacked by *Jasta* 27, which credited them to Vfw Willi Kampe and Vfw Alfred Muth. Both pilots crash-landed unhurt in British lines west of Becelaere, but both observers, Britton and 2Lt R N Bullock, were wounded.

German personnel examine DH 4 A7583, which was one of three aircraft of No 57 Sqn lost to *Jasta* 18 pilots over Roulers on 2 October 1917. The observer, 2Lt William L Inglis, was killed and pilot 2Lt C G Crane captured. Capt David S Hall and Edward Patrick Hartigan were credited with four victories during the fight, but the only *Jasta* 18 casualty was Ltn Walter Kleffel, badly wounded in the process of bringing down Crane and Inglis *(Leslie Rogers Collection via Jack Herris)*

Invalided home to serve as an administrative lieutenant, Britton was gazetted for the MC and the *Croix de Guerre*. On 28 September 1918 he resigned his commission due to failing health, dying of influenza in Balham, London, on 19 February 1919.

Another No 57 Sqn member who became a nemesis of the enemy, Alexander Roulstone was born in Nottingham on 10 October 1890, and commissioned into the 12th Battalion, Nottinghamshire and Derby Regiment, before transferring to the RFC in August 1916. On 23 March 1917 he joined No 25 Sqn, and while flying in FE 2b 7686 with 2Lt E G Green as his observer he shot down an Albatros D III in flames east of Givenchy, his victim possibly being Vfw Reinhold Wurzmann of *Jasta* 20, reportedly killed in flames near Maray. Roulstone and Green destroyed another Albatros on the 24th and Roulstone and Lt H Cotton downed another OOC on 21 May. His appointment as a flight leader in July coincided with the replacement of the 'Fees' with DH 4s, and with 2Lt L F Williams as observer Roulstone claimed an Albatros D V OOC on the 20th and a two-seater on the 22nd. On 22 August he and 2Lt D W T Fox scored another 'flamer' southeast of Carvin, although the Germans record no comparable loss. Roulstone was posted to Home Establishment on 4 September and gazetted for the MC on the 19th.

On 27 February 1918 Capt Roulstone returned to the front as a flight leader in No 57 Sqn. Flying DH 4 A7901 with Lt D F V Page, he downed an Albatros D V OOC east of Ledeghem on 13 March. Four days later he and 2Lt William Charles Venmore, a former London Fusilier with two previous victories

Hailing from Helensburgh, Dumbarton, Scotsman David Sidney Hall served in the 9th Argyll and Sutherland Highlanders before joining No 57 Sqn, with which he and 2Lt N M Pizey downed an Albatros D V on 27 July 1917. Made 'A' Flight leader, Capt Hall, with 2Lt Edward Patrick Hartigan as his observer, downed four D Vs on 2 October and a fifth on the 28th. Their DH 4 A7586 failed to return on 20 November, however, and its wreck was subsequently found at Les Alleux, with both crewmen dead (*Norman Franks*)

Born on 16 March 1884, Claude Harry Stokes came from Blackheath, southeast London. He worked as a mechanical engineer at an ore-reduction unit in Rhodesia from 1910 to June 1916, when he joined the RFC Special Reserve. Injured in No 41 Sqn, he served as an instructor in 1917 until transferred to No 57 Sqn as a captain on 2 January 1918. Flying DH 4 D8398, Stokes scored five victories between 19 June and 21 September. On 29 October his aeroplane was brought down by anti-aircraft fire over Maubeuge. The bombardier, 2Lt L H Eyles, was taken prisoner, but Stokes died of his injuries on 7 November (*Norman Franks*)

to his credit, were returning from a bombing mission over Linselles when their formation was attacked by six enemy fighters. Roulstone pulled up into an Immelmann turn and fired 50 rounds at the leader before his Vickers jammed, then swung around to allow Venmore to give the foe another 150. Last seen descending trailing a dense cloud of smoke, the 'Albatros' was credited as OOC north of Menin at 1130 hrs. Both 'Britishers' were badly wounded, but their victim turned out to be Oblt Hans Bethge, 20-victory ace and commander of *Jasta* 30, who crashed near Passchendaele in Pfalz D IIIa 5888/17 at 1130 hrs and died of his wounds shortly thereafter.

After leading flights in Nos 110 and 100 Sqns post-war Alex Roulstone left the RAF on 18 March 1920. He was residing in Loughborough as late as 1954.

— A Yank in the RFC and Two in the RAF —

Even before the United States declared war on Germany on 6 April 1917 there were Americans who joined Allied air arms – either France's via the Foreign Legion or Britain's by passing themselves off as Canadians. Although the French-serving Lafayette Flying Corps enjoyed more publicity, the only American volunteers to achieve ace status in reconnaissance or bomber aircraft did so in British service. The first, Frederick Libby, was a cowboy from Sterling, Colorado, who joined the Canadian Expeditionary Force (CEF) in 1915. From the trenches he transferred to the RFC and became an FE 2b observer in Nos 23 and 11 Sqns, with whom he was credited with ten victories between 15 July and 20 October 1916 (as recounted in Osprey Aircraft of the Aces 88 - *Pusher Aces of World War 1*).

Libby subsequently became a pilot, and on 7 March 1917 he returned to the front flying Sopwith 1½ Strutters with No 43 Sqn, adding two more victories to his tally by July. The following month saw him appointed to lead 'B' Flight in No 25 Sqn, piloting DH 4 A7543 with 2Lt D M Hills to down an Albatros D V on 8 August and a two-seater six days later for his 14th victory. On 15 September Libby transferred to the US Army Air Service (USAS), but saw no further combat. Fred Libby died in Los

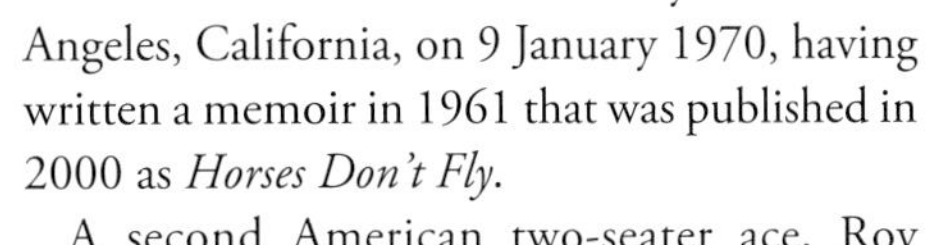

Angeles, California, on 9 January 1970, having written a memoir in 1961 that was published in 2000 as *Horses Don't Fly*.

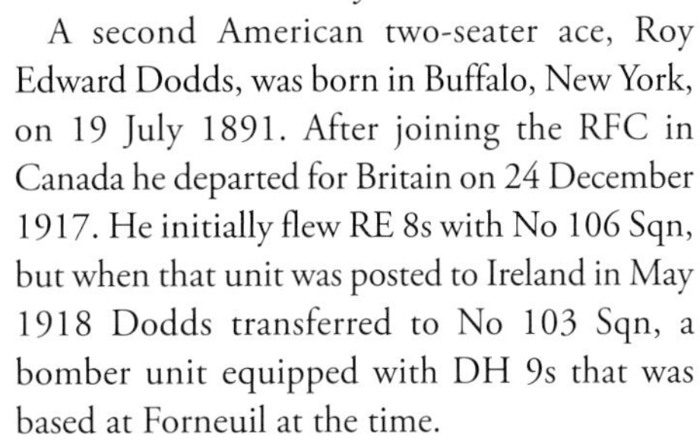

A second American two-seater ace, Roy Edward Dodds, was born in Buffalo, New York, on 19 July 1891. After joining the RFC in Canada he departed for Britain on 24 December 1917. He initially flew RE 8s with No 106 Sqn, but when that unit was posted to Ireland in May 1918 Dodds transferred to No 103 Sqn, a bomber unit equipped with DH 9s that was based at Forneuil at the time.

Arriving on 26 May, Dodds was assigned to 'C' Flight under Capt John Stevenson Stubbs – as hardened a role model as might be wished. Born on 24 September 1894 at Walton-on-the-Hill, Lancashire, Stubbs had enrolled in St Bees

Although born in Alabama on 2 November 1891, Ernest Graham Joy was a Canadian citizen and a Toronto lawyer when war broke out. A major in the CEF's 74th Battalion, he transferred to the RFC and served short stints in Nos 49 and 23 Sqns before being posted to No 57 Sqn, with which he and 2Lt Forde Leathley jointly downed seven Albatros D Vs OOC between 28 July and 20 August 1917. Posted to England the next day, Joy returned in September 1918, flying 12 missions in DH 9As with No 205 Sqn and destroying a Fokker D VII, together with 2Lt L A Drain, on 4 November. Awarded the DFC, Joy interrupted his law practice to serve in the Canadian Army during World War 2. He died in Toronto on 21 June 1993 (*Stewart Taylor via Norman Franks*)

School in 1909, but when war broke out he was in the 3rd South Lancashires, Territorial Reserve. In August 1914 he earned the Mons Ribbon and subsequently served in Egypt, before becoming a pilot in No 27 Sqn. Wounded on 9 May 1917, he subsequently instructed at Lake Down until 21 April 1918, when he was promoted to the rank of captain in the RAF and assigned to No 103 Sqn. Stubbs' usual observer, 2Lt Charles Cannon Dance, born on 25 February 1899, hailed from Forest Hill, southeast London, and had fought with the London Scottish Regiment before being seconded to the RFC on 29 August 1917 and joining No 103 Sqn on 10 April 1918.

Born in Toronto on 3 April 1888, Conrad Tolendal Lally was mayor of Wainwright, Alberta, when he enlisted in the CEF, then the RFC. On 11 April 1917 he joined No 25 Sqn as a captain, and on 7 June he and 2Lt L F Williams downed two Albatros D IIIs. After No 25 Sqn switched from FE 2bs to DH 4s, Lally flew A7477 with 2Lt Basil John Blackett, claiming an Albatros D V destroyed on 5 August and two D Vs OOC on 3 September. Blackett, from Potters Bar, went on to serve with No 18 Sqn, adding two Fokker D VIIs to his tally as bombardier to Capt Albert Gregory Waller on 30 May. Lally died in Wainwright on 5 August 1941 (*Norman Franks*)

On 20 May Stubbs and Dance, flying DH 9 A6179, scored the squadron's first victory by burning a balloon at Seclin at 1100 hrs. They were in turn shot down near Warfusée at 1125 hrs, probably by Ltn Viktor von Pressentin *Gennannt* von Rautter of *Jasta* 4, but they came down in Allied lines little the worse for wear. While bombing Roye and the railway sidings at Le Fère on 6 June, Stubbs and Dance shared one Fokker D VII in flames and another down OOC over Fretoy. During a mission to La Bassée on 4 July Dodds marked American Independence Day by sharing in a Pfalz D IIIa driven down OOC by his observer, 2Lt John B Russell. Stubbs and Dance despatched a second Pfalz in like fashion shortly thereafter.

John Bernard Russell, born in Pictou, Nova Scotia, on 5 June 1894, had joined the CEF in Ottawa on 17 May 1915, later becoming an observer. When Dance was injured in a crash on 11 July 1918, Russell became Stubbs' observer. On 31 July they were attacked by ten Fokker D VIIs, but Stubbs shot one down and Russell another, after which they descended to 1500 ft to bomb their target, a railway station. Both were awarded the DFC for this action.

On 10 August No 103 Sqn attacked Péronne railway station and two Fokkers were credited to Stubbs and Russell as OOC south of Armentières. Another two fell OOC to Dodds and his new observer, Canadian-born

One of the Sopwith 1½ Strutters flown by Capt Frederick Libby after the American, who had already scored ten victories as an observer in FE 2s, returned to the front as a pilot in No 43 Sqn. Flying Sopwith A1010, he and 2Lt J L Dickson destroyed an enemy two-seater on 6 May 1917, and in A8785 on 23 July he and 2Lt E W Pritchard sent an Albatros D III down OOC northeast of Lens (*Sally Ann March*)

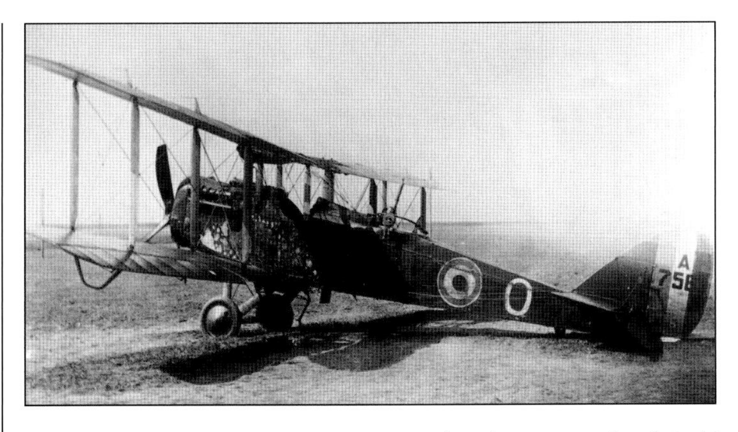

DH 4 A7563 of No 25 Sqn, in which 2Lt C J Fitzgibbon and 2Lt W Rudman MC were brought down between Valenciennes and Cambrai on 21 April 1918. Commanding 'B' Flight within the squadron, Capt Fred Libby piloted DH 4 A7543, with 2Lt D M Hills as his observer, to score his last two victories on 8 and 14 August, bringing his total to 14 (*Colin Owers*)

2Lt Irving Benfield Corey. Attacking Sainguin the next day, Dodds and Corey downed two Fokkers OOC over Estaires. Whilst bombing Lomme on the 25th the squadron was attacked by ten Fokkers and claimed five, Stubbs and Russell accounting for one destroyed and one OOC and Dodds and Corey two more OOCs.

Russell was now an ace and Dance, rejoining the squadron on 29 August, achieved that status the next day when, reunited with Stubbs for a reconnaissance mission between Bac-Saint-Maur and Armentières, he drove a Fokker down OOC. On 6 September Stubbs and Dance destroyed a Fokker west of Saint André.

Dodds was promoted to captain and given command of 'B' Flight on 30 September, and recommended for the DFC on 24 October. Six days later a Fokker OOC over Mainvault raised his and Corey's collective scores to seven, and earned Corey the DFC. Stubbs and 2Lt C G Bannerman destroyed a Fokker over Montreuil that same day (30 October), and although their DH 9 D550 was also brought down, Stubbs again alighted in Allied lines intact. Logging almost 90 sorties, including 78 over the lines, he was the highest-scoring DH 9 pilot with 11 victories, eight of which he claimed with his front gun.

Aside from on-and-off RAF Reserve duties into 1924, nothing more is known of Stubbs' career, save his death in Wrexham, Wales, on 17 October 1963. Having logged at least 64 combat sorties, Roy Dodds sold cars in Detroit post-war, and during World War 2 he served as a Link Trainer instructor for the Royal Canadian Air Force. He died in 1966.

The RAF's other American bomber ace, James Alfred Keating, was born in Chicago on 4 December 1897, joined the USAS and was attached to No 49 Sqn on 26 May 1918 to gain experience until he could get an American squadron assignment. Flying DH 9s with 26-year-old 2Lt Edward Arthur Simpson (a Londoner formerly of the Royal Irish Fusiliers) as his observer, Keating was credited with a Fokker D VII OOC on 22 July and a Pfalz D IIIa in flames on 8 August. In a 15-minute running fight the next morning they claimed two Fokkers in flames and two OOC, for which both men received the DFC and Keating was additionally awarded the Distinguished Service Cross (DSC) and Silver Star by his own army.

Another DH 9 pilot from the New World to claim multiple victories, 2Lt Arthur Rowe Spurling was born in Bermuda on 19 May 1896. Earning his Royal Aero Club certificate on 21 August, he joined No 49 Sqn in July 1918. His observer, 23-year-old Sgt Frank William Bell, was an iron and brass moulder from Cheshire who had previous combat experience following service with No 9 Sqn from November 1916 through to December 1917. Assigned DH 9 D3056, the duo first scored on 25 July with a Fokker D VII OOC over Mont Notre Dame.

On 23 August Spurling became disoriented in a cloud and was about to land when a Fokker descended on him. It was at this point that he realised that he was over a German aerodrome near Lens, with several more enemy fighters below him. In the ensuing melee Spurling claimed three of his pursuers and Bell another two, three of which they reported were burning on the ground. D3056 was badly shot up the next day, but Spurling brought it home with neither crewman hurt. He was awarded the DFC for his quintuple victory, while Bell, with 18 bombing missions behind him, was gazetted for the Distinguished Flying Medal.

Sporting unusual wheel décor, DH 9 D550 of No 103 Sqn was piloted by Capt John Stevenson Stubbs when scoring his 11th, and last, victory (a Fokker D VII) near Montreuil on 30 October. Although D550 was still operational when Stubbs was posted home on 8 November, on 6 January 1919 the aeroplane was destroyed by Lt Ronald W Jackson (who replaced Stubbs as 'B' Flight leader), with 2Lt Edward A Slater as observer, when he 'cracked it up' on landing at Ronchin (*Jack Herris*)

During World War 2 Spurling rose to the rank of group captain in RAF Transport Command and reportedly identified a Nazi spy in Canada. He subsequently ran a fleet of taxis and established the Rowe Spurling Paint Co Ltd. Moving with his wife to Guernsey in the 1970s, he died of Alzheimer's disease in England in 1984 and was buried in Bermuda.

INDEPENDENT FORCE

The withdrawal of 3 Naval Wing from Ochey in April 1917 ended Britain's first bombing effort against German industry, but the Gotha raids on London in July raised a public outcry for retribution. A concurrent report on Britain's air policy and organisation by Lt Gen Jan Christian Smuts (then a member of the British War Cabinet) determined that in 1918 the aircraft requirements of the RFC and RNAS would be fulfilled with a healthy surplus. This led to proposals that a separate, independent Air Ministry and air arm be formed, along with a strategic bombing force to strike anew at German war production.

Both recommendations were realised. On 1 April 1918 the RFC and RNAS were amalgamated into the Royal Air Force. On 6 June a separate organisation called the Independent Force was formed under Maj Gen Trenchard. The Air Ministry optimistically projected this to ultimately comprise 28 squadrons operating from the Nancy area, obliterating industrial towns one by one. What Trenchard got in June, however, were Nos 55, 99 and 104 Sqns at Azelot aerodrome for day bombing, to be joined by No 110 Sqn in August. Night bombing would be undertaken by Nos 97, 100, 115, 215 and 216 Sqns, operating Handley Page O/400s from Xaffévillers.

The day bombers of No 55 Sqn were tried-and-true DH 4s powered by 275 hp Rolls-Royce Eagle VI and VII engines that gave them a speed of 102 mph at 15,000 ft. These motors would be replaced in September by 375 hp Eagle VIIIs, raising performance to 126 mph. The remaining two units, Nos 99 and 104 Sqn, used the DH 9. This was an intended improvement on the DH 4 that relocated the pilot aft, back-to-back with his observer for better cooperation, and boasted 4.5 hours endurance. Its Siddeley Puma engines, however, produced only 230 hp in practice for a 105 mph top speed. Furthermore, they were chronically unreliable.

The day bombers' payload consisted of either one 230-lb Mk III bomb under the fuselage or, more often, two 112-lb Mk Is under the wings. Attacks on aerodromes involved 40-lb incendiary or 20- to 25-lb explosive Cooper bombs. Such puny ordnance required massed formations to be

Flying DH 9 D3056 with No 49 Sqn, 2Lt Arthur Rowe Spurling became Bermuda's sole ace of World War 1, including a quintuple victory on 23 August 1918. While leading Ferry Command in 1942 Flt Lt Spurling learned from a civilian employee that she had been offered a $100 a week job in California by one of his men, English-born Brian Percy Pettit, to report enemy aircraft movements to him. Pettit turned out to be a spy and radio operator for the German Gestapo (*BermudaOnline.org*)

effective, but these were difficult to maintain given the speed discrepancy between the DH 4 and DH 9.

Opposing the bombers was a well developed communication network that controlled both heavy flak batteries and nine *Kampfeinsitzer Staffeln* (*Kests*), equipped with anything from second-line fighters to specialised interceptors such as the fast-climbing Siemens-Schuckert D III and D IV. Several *Jagdstaffeln* were also occasionally moved in to protect the targeted towns. All this meant plenty of action and painful attrition for the bomber crews, as well as the usual spate of accredited victories out of proportion to actual German losses. The only Independent Force unit to produce aces, however, was No 104 Sqn under Maj John Charles Quinnell.

The first mission on 6 June, against factories and the train station and barracks at Coblenz, was carried out by No 55 Sqn with fair success, but six of the eleven DH 9s that No 99 Sqn sent to Thionville dropped out with engine trouble. The first raid by No 104 Sqn, on the railway station in Metz, on 8 June was completed by nine of the twelve DH 9s despatched by the unit under the leadership of Capt J B Home-Hay.

Jeffrey Batters Home-Hay was born in Alloa, Scotland, on 31 January 1890 and subsequently emigrated to Canada with his widowed mother, three sisters and two brothers. When war broke out he was commissioned in the 7th Reserve Battalion, Argyll and Sutherland Highlanders, later transferring to the RFC. Obtaining his Royal Aero Club certificate on 10 July 1916, Home-Hay joined No 53 Sqn in February 1917 and earned the MC for observation work. In May 1918 he was transferred to No 104 Sqn.

Home-Hay led a strike on Hagondange railway station and nearby factories on 7 June, although six of his twelve DH 9s retired prior to reaching the target. One aeroplane, crewed by Lt R J Gammon and 2Lt P E Appleby, took 11 photographs that revealed two hits on factory buildings and one on a train.

Squadronmate and fellow ace Richard John Gammon was born on 5 January 1897. Subsequently studying engineering at Chiswick Polytechnic, he lived in Southall, Middlesex, before the war. Having served as an instructor with No 4 Auxiliary School of Aerial Gunnery, Gammon joined No 104 Sqn on 1 May 1918. His observer once in the frontline was Percival Ewart Appleby, who was born on 27 June 1894 in Port-la-Tour, Nova Scotia. He had served in No 1 Field Ambulance in France and Salonika prior to being commissioned in the King's Royal Rifles on 26 April 1917. On 27 January 1918 Appleby became an observer in No 10 Kite Balloon Section, before transferring, per his request, to No 104 Sqn on 17 May.

On 30 June Capt Home-Hay led 11 aeroplanes on an 80-mile mission to the barracks and railway station at Landau – two DH 9s turned back with engine trouble. Two German two-seaters and three Albatros scouts that had followed the formation for some time eventually attacked at 0730 hrs, disengaging near the target as their flak batteries took over but resuming their attack as the bombers headed home. *Jasta* 70 joined in, with Vfw Heinrich Krüger shooting a DH 9 down in flames, killing American Lt William L Deetjen and South African 2Lt Montague H Cole, while Uffz Dörr wounded 2Lt Oscar J Lange and Sgt V G McCabe, who, nevertheless, made a pancake landing in Allied lines. No 104 Sqn in turn claimed three enemy fighters OOC, including one credited to Home-Hay and his observer, 2Lt C C Blizard.

Born on 21 November 1897, Charles Cecil Blizard hailed from Putney, southwest London, and was a student at Mill Hill School from 1910 to 1915, when he joined the 20th Battalion of the Middlesex Regiment. Attending the 4th Army Signals School in 1917, Blizard was posted to No 104 Sqn on 7 April 1918.

On 1 July ten DH 9s targeted the railway station at Karthaus, although only seven reached it and two were lost to enemy fighters, their crews being captured. The British claimed three German scouts in return, including an Albatros seen to spin down and crash after Appleby fired 90 rounds at it – his and Gammon's first victory. During a six-aeroplane mission to the railway complex at Metz-Sablon five days later Blizard fired 30 rounds at an attacking fighter and saw it go down trailing smoke.

Karthaus was the target for 14 No 104 Sqn DH 9s on 1 August, but due to mist over the target they went for the Treves railway station instead. Albatros and Pfalz scouts attacked over Boulez aerodrome, one of which was driven down OOC by Lts B H Stretton and W E Jackson. A Pfalz was also sent down in a vertical spin by Sgt William Harrop, bombardier to 2Lt G H B Smith, his victim being seen to crash. Finally, Gammon and Appleby were also credited with a Pfalz destroyed after the latter had fired more than 100 rounds into one that duly crashed. The unit lost the DH 9 crewed by Canadian Lt Walter H Goodale and American Lt Lee C Prentice, however, both men being killed. 2Lt Alfred Haines was also wounded, but he managed to land his DH 9 on the Allied side of the frontline. Ltn Kurt Seit of *Jasta* 80b and Uffz Hans Heinrich Marwede of *Jasta* 67 each received credit for destroying a DH 9.

George Henry Benjamin Smith was yet another DH 9 ace from No 104 Sqn. Born on 20 August 1899 in Camberwell, southeast London, he had served as a clerk prior to joining the RFC. His observer, Sgt W Harrop, had been a Pioneer in the 95th Field Company, Royal Engineers, before switching to the RFC and eventually being assigned to No 104 Sqn.

On 11 August the unit had been ordered to target the Benz factory at Mannheim, but when it was obscured by cloud cover Maj Quinnell led his 11 DH 9s in an attack on the railway station at Karlsrühe instead. Although a DH 9 was downed by Ltn d R Sauermann of *Jasta* 70, its crew being captured, five German fighters were in turn claimed by No 104 Sqn, including a Pfalz to Home-Hay and his observer, Sgt William Thomas Smith. The latter, a 21-year-old from Maida Vale who had also previously served in the Royal Engineers, had claimed an Albatros D V exactly one year earlier whilst serving as an observer with No 45 Sqn. Smith had received a Distinguished Conduct Medal during his time with this unit after he had climbed out onto the wing of his Sopwith 1½ Strutter and taken control of the aircraft when its wounded pilot, Capt Ian McAllister Moffat Pender, fainted. *Jasta* 70 reported Ltn Straube as wounded in action following the 11 August clash.

This raid had caused considerable damage, and Maj Quinnell received the following telegram from Trenchard;

'A great day for you and 104. It will help the battle up north. It showed determination, pluck and good leaderhip. Well done all!'

Home-Hay led 12 aeroplanes aloft the following day with orders to again attack Mannheim. One aeroplane had to turn back and 23 German fighters attacked the remaining bombers just four miles into enemy

Hailing from Putney, southwest London, Charles Cecil Blizard joined No 104 Sqn on 7 April 1918, sharing in four victories with Capt J B Home-Hay and a fifth with 2Lt P Hopkinson (on 6 November 1918). He left the RAF on 19 June 1919 (*Norman Franks*)

Born in Kircudbrightshire, Scotland, 2Lt Arthur Rullion Rattray saw action with the Royal Indian Marines before scoring five victories as an observer in No 104 Sqn. Serving in the Royal Indian Navy during World War 2, Rear Admiral Rattray was knighted in 1948 and died in Camberley, Surrey, on 10 August 1966, aged 75 (*Imperial War Museum*)

territory after crossing the frontline at Schirmeck. Home-Hay flew head-on at a Fokker D VII, firing 50 rounds from 100 yards and watching it spin down and break up. Smith and Harrop claimed two destroyed and one OOC, while 2Lt G Pickup's observer, Lt Arthur B Rattray, was credited with two Pfalz, as was the team of Lts Horace P Wells and John J Redfield. Also claiming an enemy aeroplane OOC was 2Lt William Eric Bottrill. Born in Burton-on-Trent, Staffordshire, on 26 September 1892, he had moved to Hamilton, Ontario, working as a salesman and stockbroker before joining the CEF and being sent to the RFC as an observer. With Lt Desmond Phillip Pogson as his pilot, Bottrill described what happened when they came under attack at 0725 hrs;

'One enemy aircraft painted with gold spangled upper planes and black crosses with silver edges dived at B Flight [second formation] and fired at the machine on our left rear. The whole formation fired their Lewis guns at it, and I did not see the enemy aircraft re-appear. Later, several enemy aircraft attacked from the right rear, and I saw Lt Redfield's tracers striking two separate enemy aircraft – these went down vertically out of control. One enemy aircraft attacked Redfield and then came past myself, and I fired a long burst as he made a turn, tracer hitting him in the engine and fuselage. He then nose-dived, stalled and ended up spinning in.'

This 40-minute running battle quickly convinced Home-Hay to abandon Mannheim and lead No 104 Sqn to Haguenau aerodrome instead. The unit was subsequently credited with four enemy aeroplanes destroyed and two OOC, but it lost two DH 9s and their crews, who were taken prisoner. These machines were credited to Ltn Kurt Monnington and Offz Stv Richard Schleichhardt of *Jasta* 18.

Clouds, flak, fighters and its photo-reconnaissance aeroplane returning prematurely due to engine trouble resulted in No 104 Sqn's 13 August attack on the railway junction at Ehrang being rerouted to the railway workshops at Thionville. In what proved to be a black day for the unit, four DH 9s were lost with all crewmen killed. Two fell to Ltn Monnington of *Jasta* 18 and the remaining pair to flak and a midair collision. Home-Hays' observer, Sgt Smith, was credited with a D V OOC and a second Albatros scout destroyed over Corny. While testing his Lewis gun prior to being engaged by enemy fighters, Sgt Harrop found the weapon's striker to be broken. Unperturbed, when his machine was targeted by a German scout Harrop managed to drive away his assailant by firing a Very pistol at him!

On 15 August Maj Quinnell led 12 DH 9s – one of which dropped out – along with four No 99 Sqn aeroplanes against Bühl aerodrome, where a Gotha unit was based. In addition to one bomber blown up and a hangar damaged, 2Lt Jackson, Sgts Harrop and Smith and Lt Redfield were each credited with a Pfalz OOC. Home-Hay's damaged DH 9 fell out of formation, but he brought it and Sgt Smith safely back to Serres.

Seven days later Home-Hay led 12 aeroplanes on a 115-mile raid on the Badische Analine Soda Fabrik Werke in Mannheim, only to come under attack once more over Schirmeck. Rattray, observer to 2Lt J W Pope, drove down a Pfalz, which was seen to catch fire just before it force landed. Bottrill, again seated behind Lt Pogson, fixed a broken extractor on his Lewis gun in time to down an enemy in flames. However, he also saw Home-Hay's DH 9, hit while Smith was suffering from a gun stoppage, go down emitting smoke and steam. Bottrill tied a large

Born in Scotland but living in Canada when war broke out, Jeffrey Batter Home-Hay joined No 53 Sqn in February 1917 and was awarded the MC. In May 1918 he joined No 104 Sqn, Independent Force, scoring seven victories and earning a DFC on 21 September. He was not around to receive it, however, having been brought down with his observer, Sgt William Thomas Smith, during a raid on Mannheim on 22 August, both men being captured (*Norman Franks*)

handkerchief to his Scarff ring to indicate that Pogson was taking charge, and they led four other DH 9s back to Azelot. Pogson was awarded the DFC following this mission, which had been a disaster for No 104 Sqn.

The unit had lost seven DH 9s, with two ace teams, Home-Hay and William Smith and George Smith and Harrop, among the 11 personnel who had been captured. In addition to one pilot and two observers dying in enemy lines, Lt P C Saxby returned with 2Lt William Moorhouse slain by flak fragments.

Among the Germans involved in the slaughter were Offz Stv Eduard Prime and Ltn Hans Jungwirth of *Jasta* 78b. Prime, who brought down the American team of Wells and Redfield in D2917, landed nearby, protected his prisoners from angry civilians and helped apply a tourniquet to Redfield's thigh wound. He later flew over the lines to drop their identity discs with an attached message that noted both men were 'Quite well'.

Withdrawn for two weeks so as to make good its losses, No 104 Sqn resumed operations on 2 September with a return attack on Bühl aerodrome. Gammon, now a captain, led 12 DH 9s back to the Badische Aneline Soda Fabrik Werke at Mannheim on the 7th, with two aeroplanes dropping out due to engine trouble and the rest being intercepted over Saverne. Gammon's observer, Appleby, claimed a Hannover destroyed, as the unit, joining No 99 Sqn, pressed on against opposition from *Jastas* 3 and 80b and *Kest* 1a. The German pilots brought down three DH 9s, with four aircrew being killed or mortally wounded and two captured. A fourth aeroplane force landed in Allied territory and another observer, Sgt Walter E Reast, succumbed to his wounds. Again sustaining heavy losses, No 104 Sqn was credited with five adversaries, including a 'Pfalz D III' for Gammon and Appleby. *Kest* 1a's CO, Oblt Rudolf Nebel, returned with 29 holes in his Fokker D VII and Fw-Ltn Schiller was badly wounded.

Returning to the fray, No 104 Sqn bombed the railway complex at Metz-Sablon on 13 and 14 September. On the latter occasion Capt Ewart J Garland was leading the second formation when he spotted a straggling No 99 Sqn DH 9 under attack by six Pfalz scouts and came to its aid, his observer, Bottrill, sending one German down to crash near Metz.

Metz-Sablon was again the target on the 15th, but this time the opposition came from *Jasta* 15, whose Ltns Hugo Schäfer and Georg von Hantelmann and Vfw Theodor Weischer brought down three DH 9s, with three dead and three captured. Another observer, 2Lt Wilfred E Jackson, died of wounds after returning, and both flight leaders, Garland and Gammon, force landed in Allied lines. One positive to emerge from this mission was that the latter pilot and his observer, Appleby, were credited with an ace-making fifth victory – probably Ltn Johannes Klein, who was wounded.

No 104 Sqn returned to Metz-Sablon on 23 October, during which it lost one aeroplane and another force landed just in Allied lines, as did a DH 9 from No 99 Sqn. These victories were credited to Ltn Prahlow of *Kest* 3, Vfw Trautmann of *Jasta* 64w and Ltn Monnington of *Jasta* 18. Enemy fighters were in turn claimed by the crews of Garland and Bottrill and Lt J H Cuthbertson and Rattray.

An attack on Jametz aerodrome six days later drew the inevitable spirited welcome, with a DH 9 going down in flames, but Bottrill fired at a Pfalz and saw it break up and Rattray sent a Fokker D VII spinning OOC. During a strike on Bühl on 6 November No 104 Sqn lost two aeroplanes to Ltn Hans Nülle and Uffz Krüchelsdorf of *Jasta* 39, but its crews in turn claimed three successes. One was credited to Lt Blizard who now sat behind 2Lt Hopkinson, belatedly adding him to the squadron's lengthening tally of aces.

In spite of its grisly losses No 104 Sqn flew sorties to the last, bombing Morhange aerodrome on 10 November. That same day Garland and Bottrill flew newly arrived twin-engined Airco DH 10 F1867, as described by the former in his diary;

'I took up the DH 10 and went to bomb Sarrebourg aerodrome on my own. I'd dropped my bombs and was coming back at 100 mph when four scouts dived around us. Bottrill let off a few bursts from his double-barrell [sic] Lewis, and suddenly we realised they were French SPADs! Lucky we didn't shoot them down or they shoot us, as the DH 10 was not known to them at the time and the SPADs undoubtedly mistook us for a Hun bomber. The SPAD chaps didn't report us for firing at them as far as we know, so all's well that ends well! What might have made things worse is that I was not supposed to take the DH 10 on a job but wanted to use it "on active service" on the last day of the war.'

Receiving the DFC from King George V, William Bottrill left the RAF on 13 January 1919, but served on various army medical boards expediting the return of Canadian servicemen from overseas. Serving again in World War 2, he retired as a colonel in the local Dundas Regiment. He died of a stroke in Dundas, Ontario, on 6 October 1971.

Post-war Percy Appleby became a farmer, ran a small business and was a music teacher, before serving as an RCAF recruiting officer during World War 2. He died of a stroke in May 1968.

Jeffrey Home-Hay also became a farmer after his release from prison. In 1920 he took part in the first trans-Canada flight from Halifax to Vancouver. He later flew an airliner for Prairie Airways on its Winnipeg-Saskatoon-Moose Jaw-Regina service. At one point Home-Hay was the oldest Canadian still flying, prior to retiring to his farm at Kelington, Saskatchewan, in 1952. He passed away there in the summer of 1956.

Airco DH 10 F1874 was of the same production batch as F1867, which, delivered to No 104 Sqn, carried out the new twin-engined bomber's only wartime sortie on 10 November 1918, crewed by Capt Ewart J Garland and five-victory observer ace 2Lt William E Bottrill (*RAF Museum*)

YANKEE SALMSONS

When the USAS began combat operations in the spring of 1918 its reconnaissance units were subdivided into two categories. Most squadrons were involved in corps observation (short-range tactical sorties over or near the frontlines), but the 9th, 24th and 91st Aero Squadrons were army observation units, conducting more strategically minded missions deep behind enemy lines.

The corps observation units were initially equipped with an assortment of aeroplanes deemed to be surplus to requirements by the French, including ARs (whose initials the Americans claimed stood for 'Antique Rattletraps'), Sopwith 1A2s and SPAD XIs and XVIs. By August, however, they were beginning to standardise around two up-to-date aircraft types, namely the French-supplied Salmson 2A2 and the British-designed, American-built Liberty DH 4. Salmsons were also issued to the 24th and 91st Aero Squadrons for army observation, while the 9th received Breguet 14A2s for the nocturnal missions that it usually flew.

Although both the Breguet and the DH 4, with its 400 hp Liberty engine, performed well in the reconnaissance role, most Americans reserved their admiration for the Salmson 2A2. While the freakish Salmson-Moineau SM 1 was proving a failure, Salmson's chief engineer Georges Canton had been working on an aeroplane with performance which surpassed that of the Sopwith 1A2s the company had been building under licence. The result was a conventional looking but efficient two-seat biplane powered by Salmson's 260 hp Canton-Unné 9Z nine-cylinder water-cooled radial engine. From its acceptance for production in June 1917, Salmson subsequently built 2200 examples, with a further 1000

Capt Everett R Cook (right) stands beside his Salmson 2A2, with his five victories marked on the white knight's shield. In the observer's pit is 2Lt William T Badham, who was also credited with five victories by the end of the war (*Everett R Cook*)

manufactured by subcontractors Latécoère, Hanriot and Compagnie Général Omnibus (CGO).

The 2A2's two 100-litre fuel tanks, held in cradles in the lower fuselage between the pilot and the observer's cockpits, were covered in wire mesh and lined with 1/8th of an inch thick sheets of sponge rubber that would seal the hole left by a bullet. 'There is no record of a Salmson ever having caught fire', claimed Everett Cook of the 91st Aero Squadron. 'In combat we soon learned that if a bullet hit the gas tank the wire mesh slowed the round down and the flame it caused by friction was extinguished when the bullet passed through the rubber covering of the gas tank, thus eliminating the main reasons for an aeroplane being set on fire. I know of no other aeroplane that had this type of construction at that time. Fear of fire was probably the greatest obstacle one had to get over, and this aeroplane built up great confidence'.

The Salmson's 115 mph maximum speed was not a world-beater, but it had a good rate of climb up to 20,000 ft and exceptional manoeuvrability for a two-seater. 'In a dive we could get up to 250 mph', Cook wrote. The only complaint crews had concerned the distance between pilot and observer, which somewhat hampered communication and cooperation, and that there was only room for 48 photographic plates at a time. Those faults aside, the Salmson 2A2 was rated as one of the best Allied reconnaissance aeroplanes of the war. *(text continues on page 59)*

Capt Victor Strahm scored five victories, some of which were claimed in concert with the 91st Aero Squadron's ordnance officer, 1Lt Thomas M Jervey, who volunteered to serve as observer on a number of missions (*Courtesy of Ray Buckberry*)

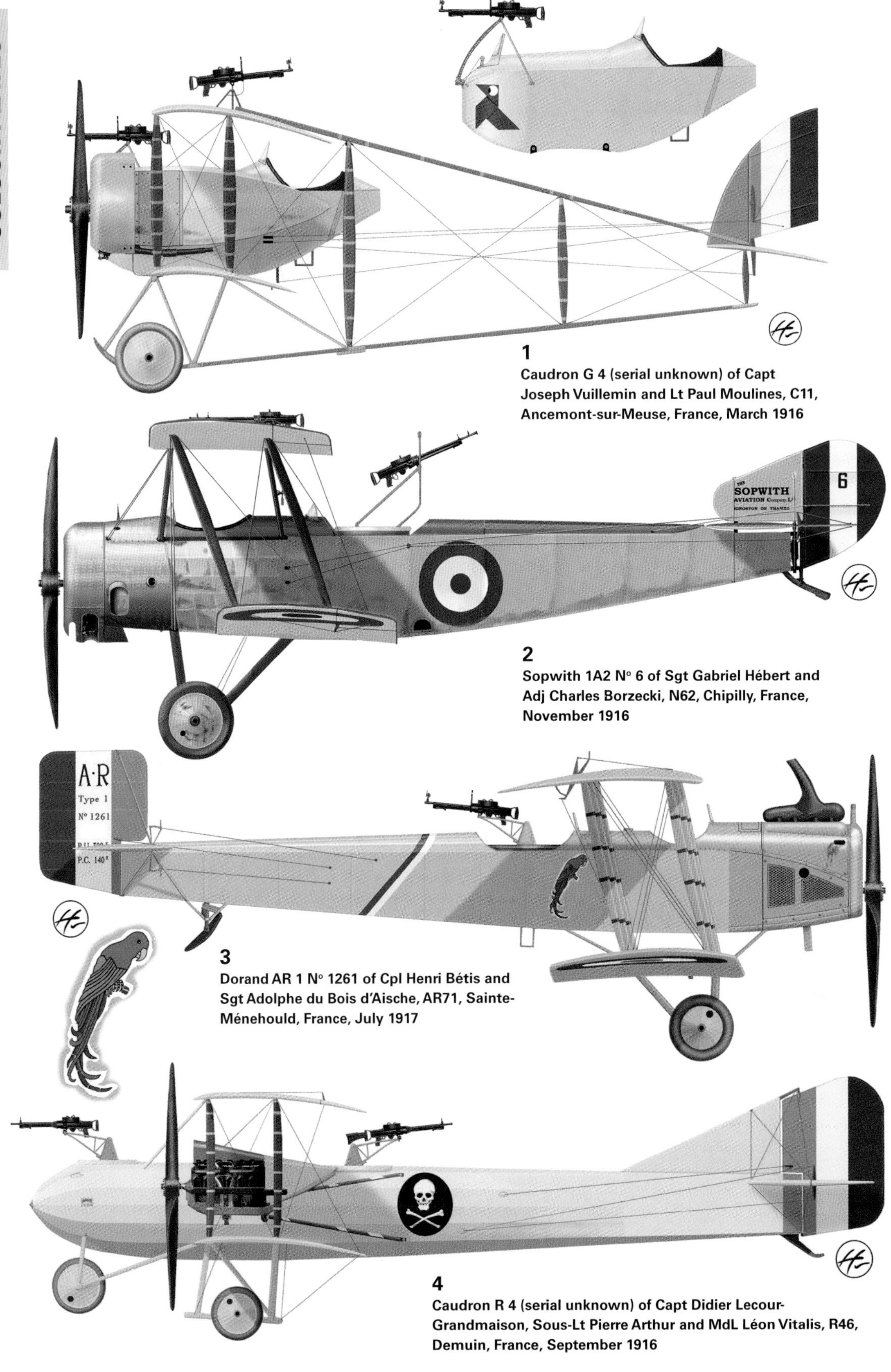

1
Caudron G 4 (serial unknown) of Capt Joseph Vuillemin and Lt Paul Moulines, C11, Ancemont-sur-Meuse, France, March 1916

2
Sopwith 1A2 N° 6 of Sgt Gabriel Hébert and Adj Charles Borzecki, N62, Chipilly, France, November 1916

3
Dorand AR 1 N° 1261 of Cpl Henri Bétis and Sgt Adolphe du Bois d'Aische, AR71, Sainte-Ménehould, France, July 1917

4
Caudron R 4 (serial unknown) of Capt Didier Lecour-Grandmaison, Sous-Lt Pierre Arthur and MdL Léon Vitalis, R46, Demuin, France, September 1916

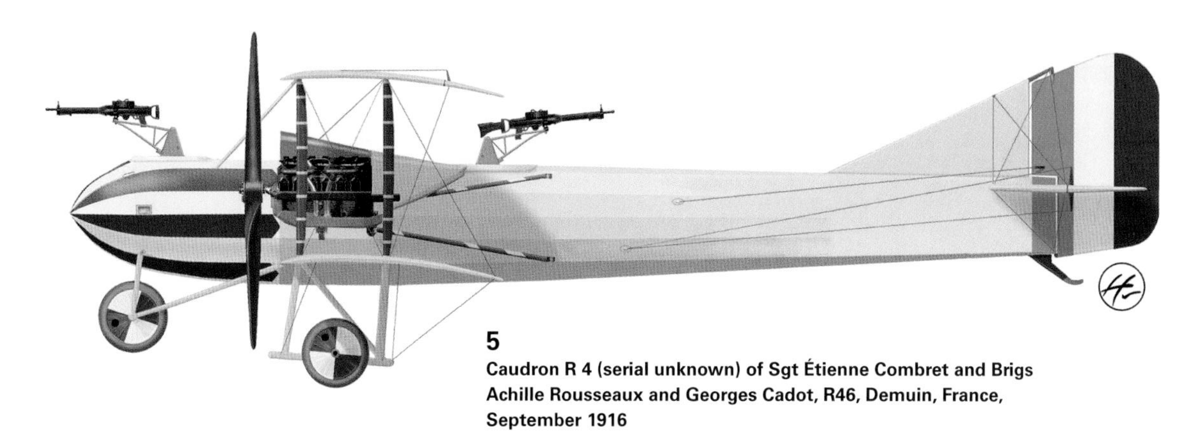

5
Caudron R 4 (serial unknown) of Sgt Étienne Combret and Brigs Achille Rousseaux and Georges Cadot, R46, Demuin, France, September 1916

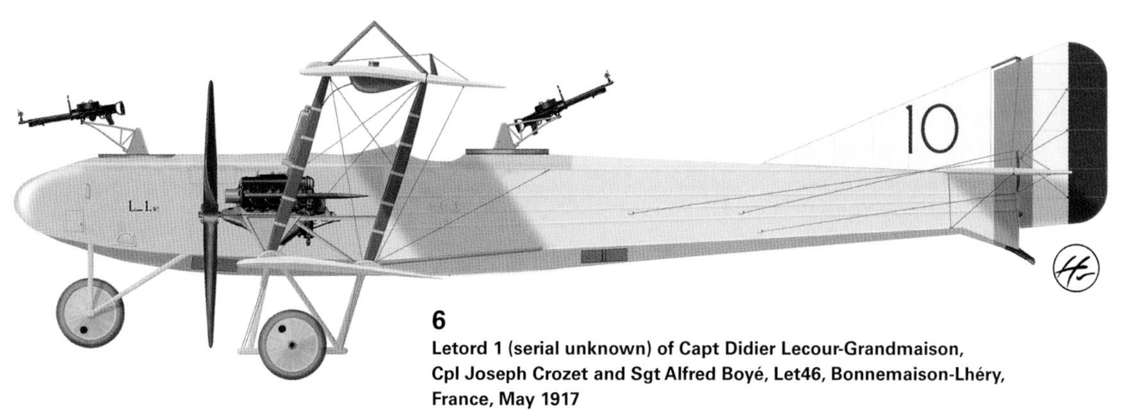

6
Letord 1 (serial unknown) of Capt Didier Lecour-Grandmaison, Cpl Joseph Crozet and Sgt Alfred Boyé, Let46, Bonnemaison-Lhéry, France, May 1917

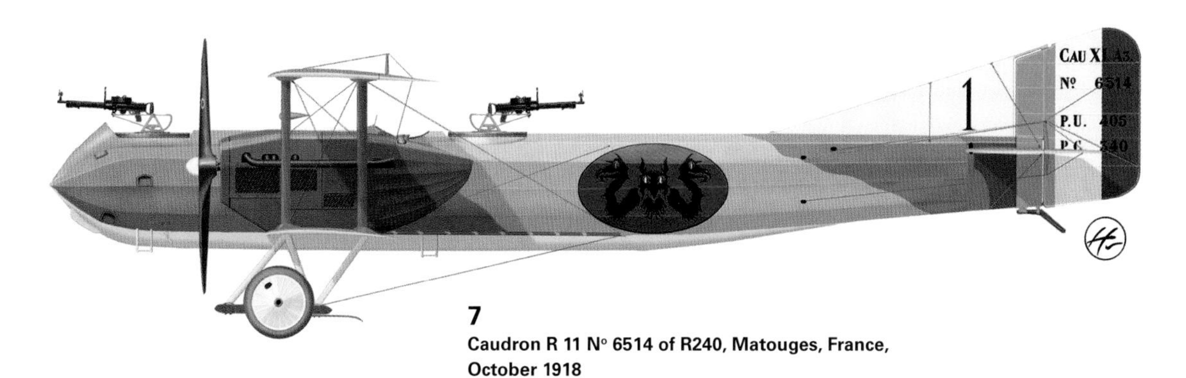

7
Caudron R 11 N° 6514 of R240, Matouges, France, October 1918

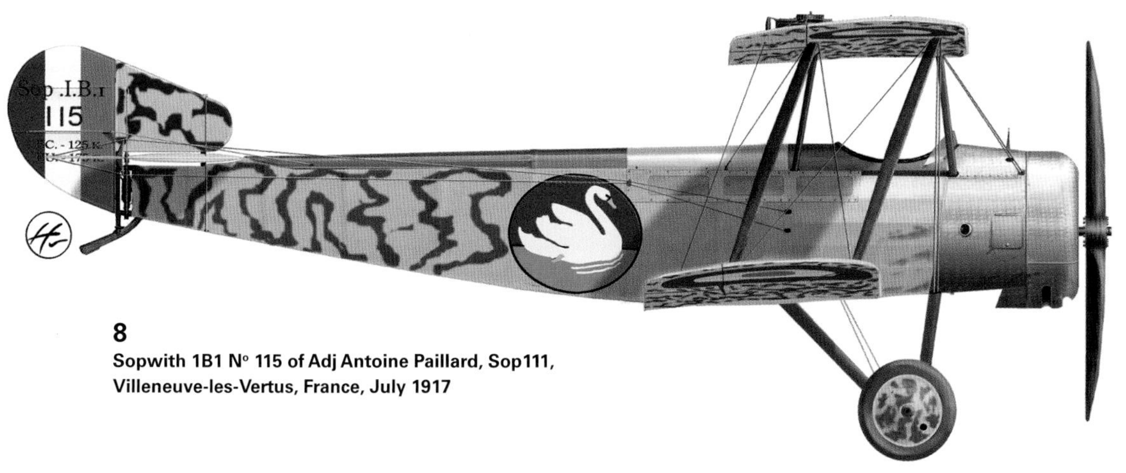

8
Sopwith 1B1 N° 115 of Adj Antoine Paillard, Sop111, Villeneuve-les-Vertus, France, July 1917

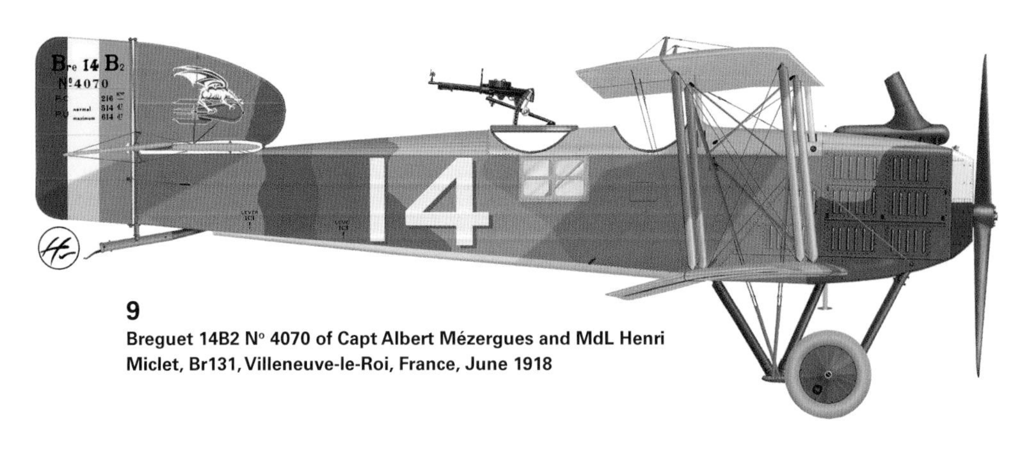

9

Breguet 14B2 N° 4070 of Capt Albert Mézergues and MdL Henri Miclet, Br131, Villeneuve-le-Roi, France, June 1918

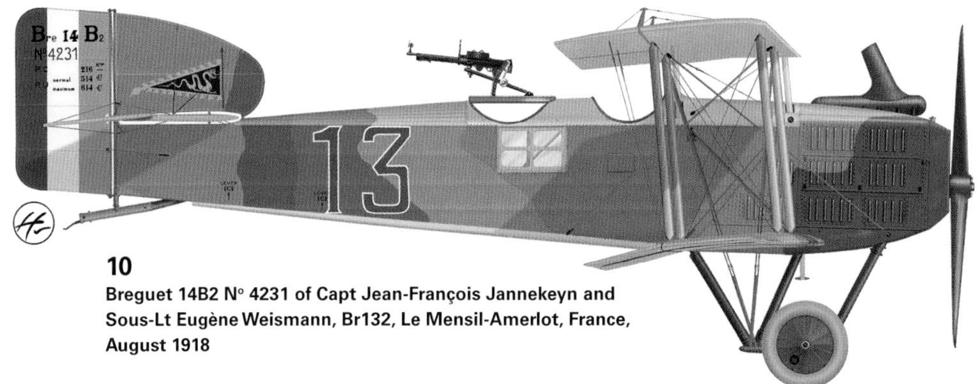

10

Breguet 14B2 N° 4231 of Capt Jean-François Jannekeyn and Sous-Lt Eugène Weismann, Br132, Le Mensil-Amerlot, France, August 1918

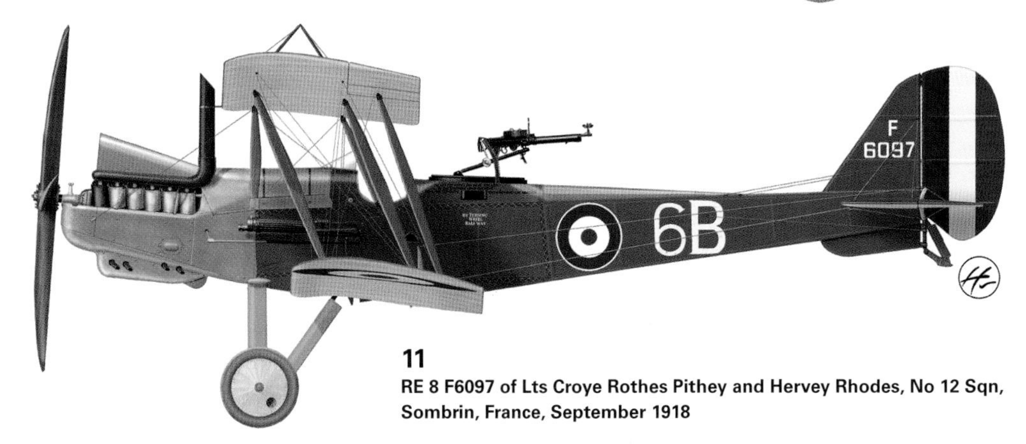

11

RE 8 F6097 of Lts Croye Rothes Pithey and Hervey Rhodes, No 12 Sqn, Sombrin, France, September 1918

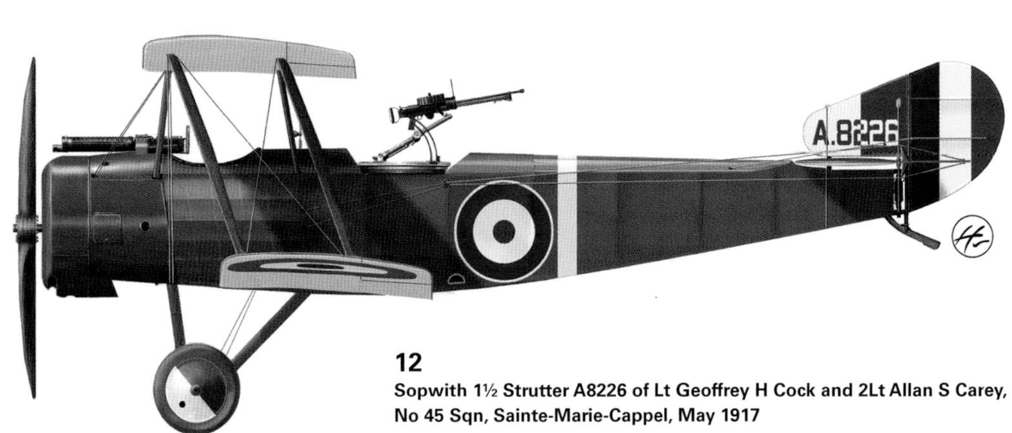

12

Sopwith 1½ Strutter A8226 of Lt Geoffrey H Cock and 2Lt Allan S Carey, No 45 Sqn, Sainte-Marie-Cappel, May 1917

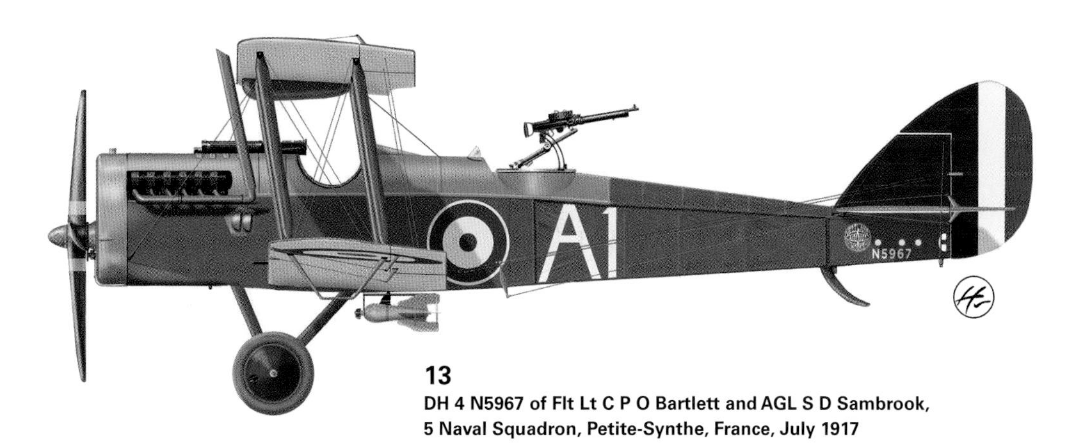

13

DH 4 N5967 of Flt Lt C P O Bartlett and AGL S D Sambrook, 5 Naval Squadron, Petite-Synthe, France, July 1917

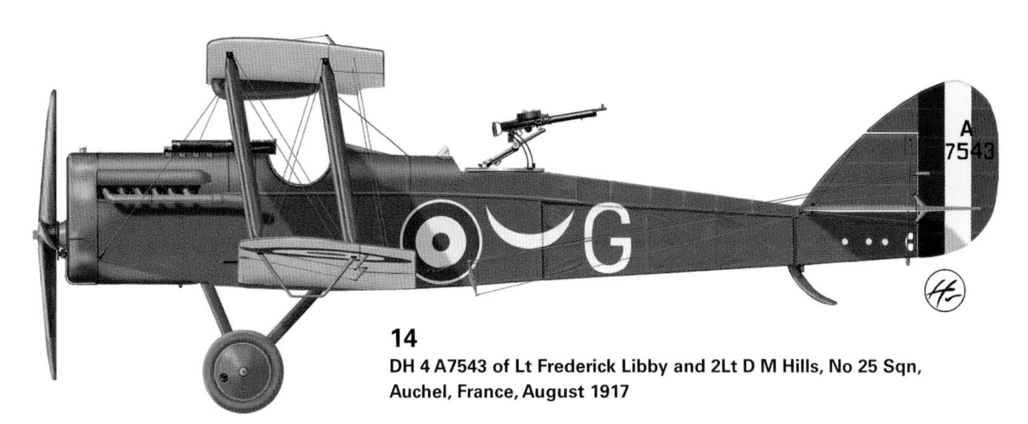

14

DH 4 A7543 of Lt Frederick Libby and 2Lt D M Hills, No 25 Sqn, Auchel, France, August 1917

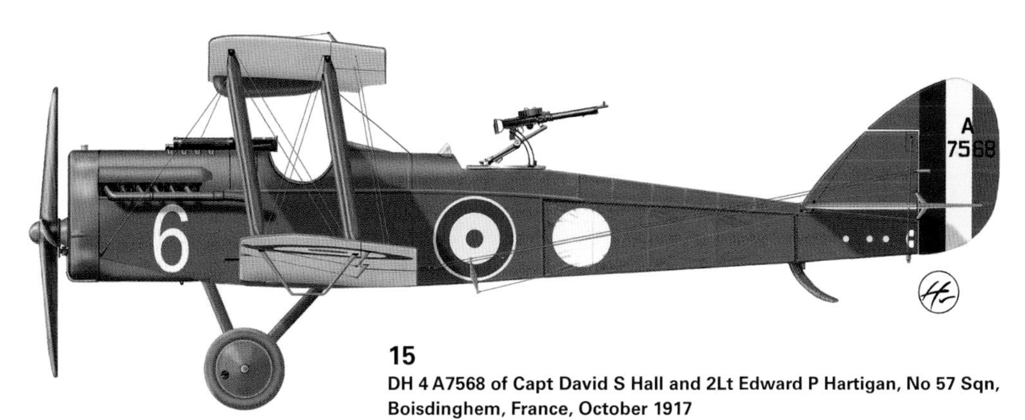

15

DH 4 A7568 of Capt David S Hall and 2Lt Edward P Hartigan, No 57 Sqn, Boisdinghem, France, October 1917

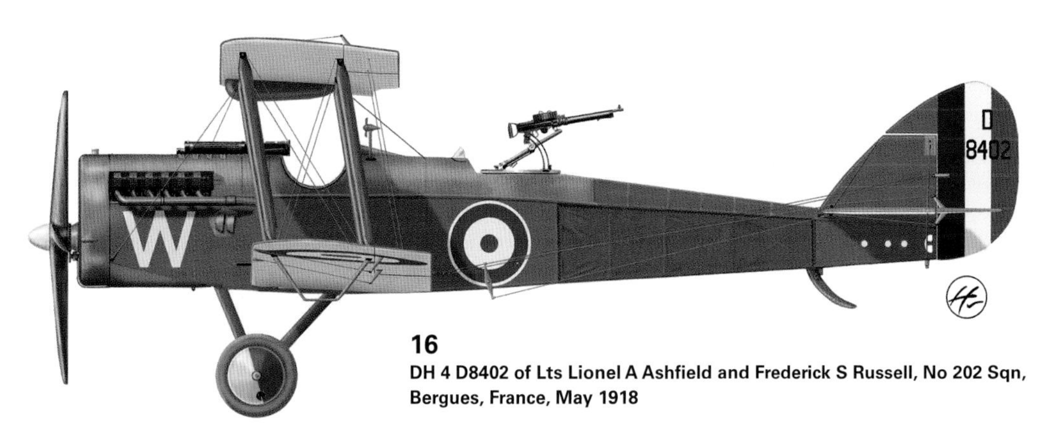

16

DH 4 D8402 of Lts Lionel A Ashfield and Frederick S Russell, No 202 Sqn, Bergues, France, May 1918

17
DH 9 C6114 of Lts Allan H Curtis and Philip T Holligan, No 49 Sqn, Petite-Synthe, France, April 1918

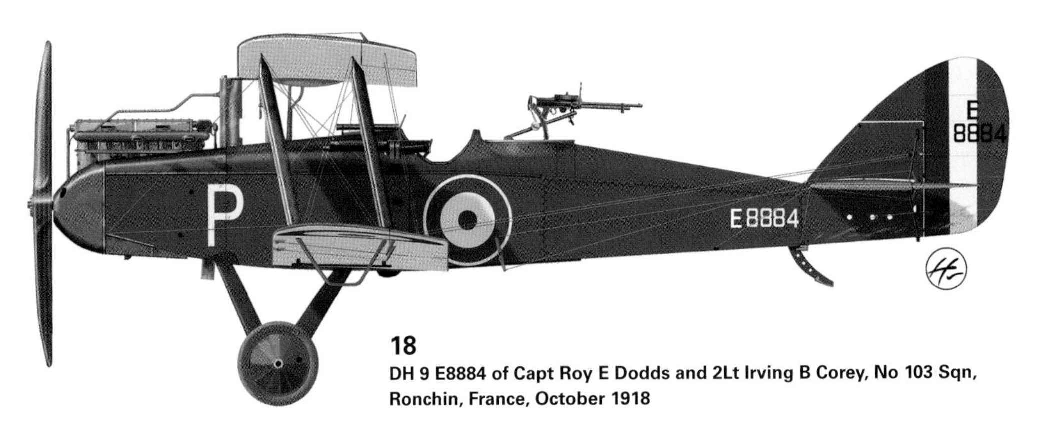

18
DH 9 E8884 of Capt Roy E Dodds and 2Lt Irving B Corey, No 103 Sqn, Ronchin, France, October 1918

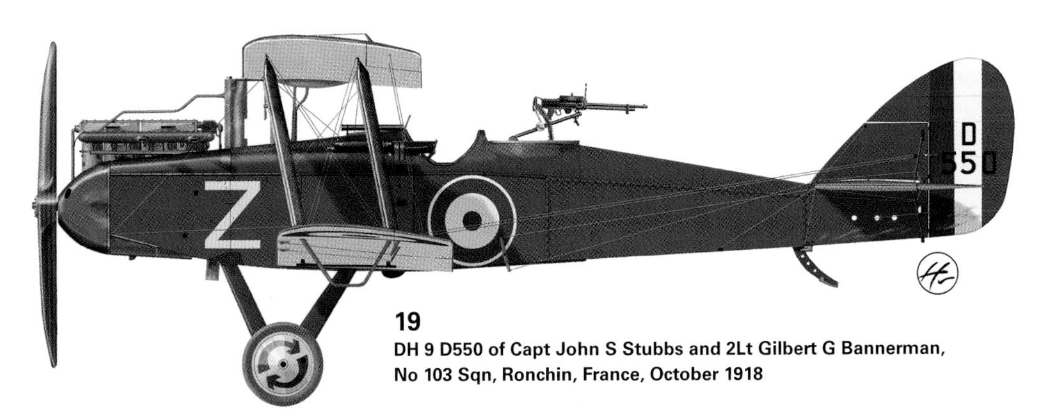

19
DH 9 D550 of Capt John S Stubbs and 2Lt Gilbert G Bannerman, No 103 Sqn, Ronchin, France, October 1918

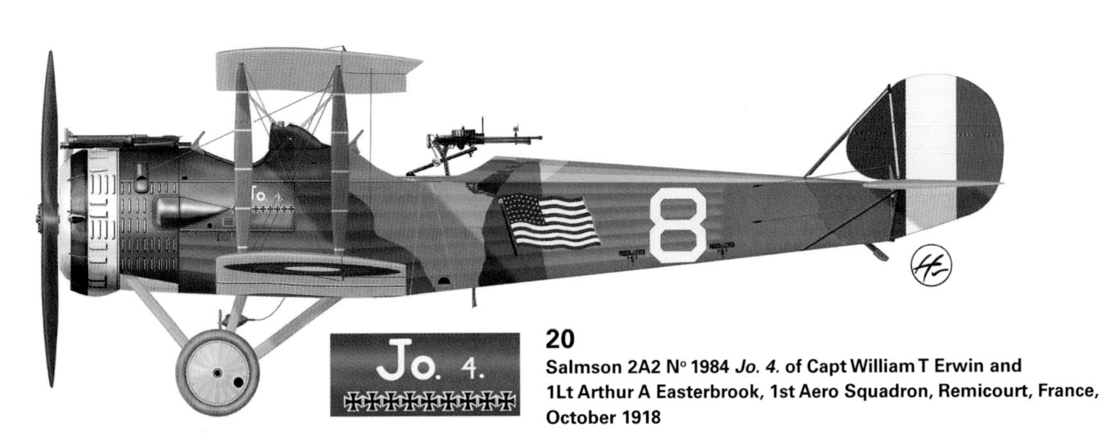

20
Salmson 2A2 N° 1984 *Jo. 4.* of Capt William T Erwin and 1Lt Arthur A Easterbrook, 1st Aero Squadron, Remicourt, France, October 1918

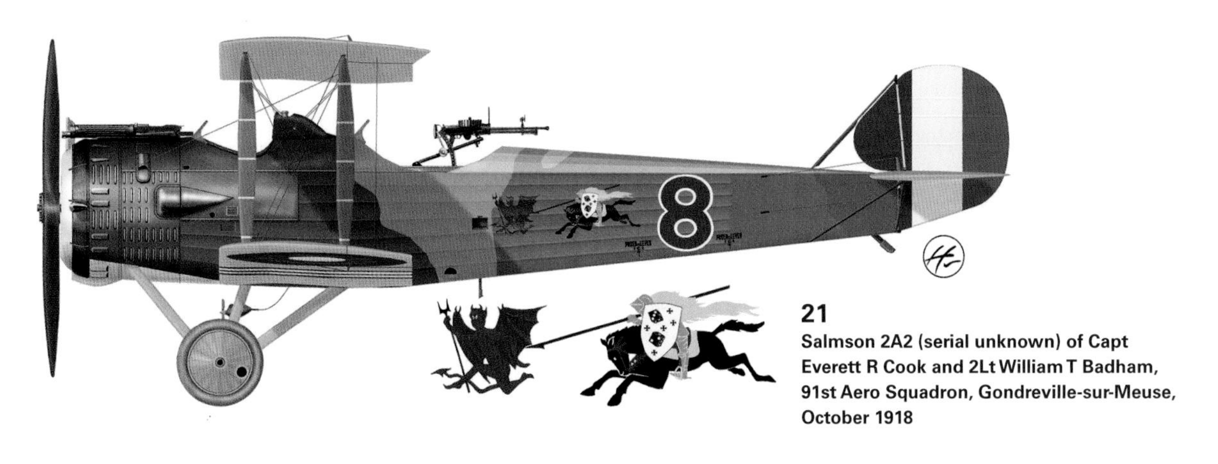

21
Salmson 2A2 (serial unknown) of Capt Everett R Cook and 2Lt William T Badham, 91st Aero Squadron, Gondreville-sur-Meuse, October 1918

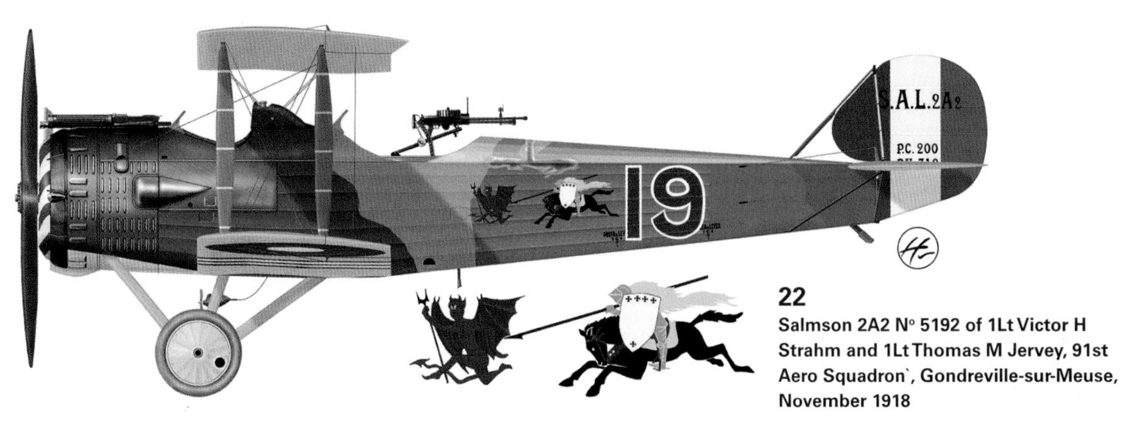

22
Salmson 2A2 Nº 5192 of 1Lt Victor H Strahm and 1Lt Thomas M Jervey, 91st Aero Squadron`, Gondreville-sur-Meuse, November 1918

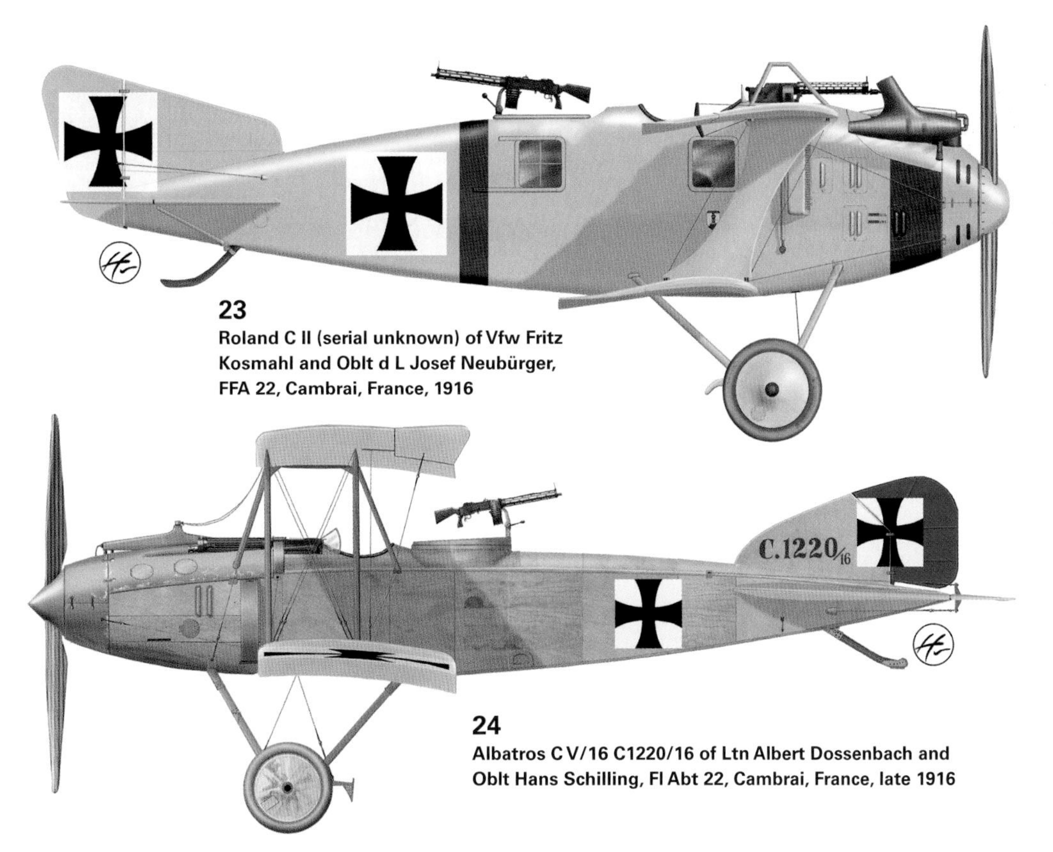

23
Roland C II (serial unknown) of Vfw Fritz Kosmahl and Oblt d L Josef Neubürger, FFA 22, Cambrai, France, 1916

24
Albatros C V/16 C1220/16 of Ltn Albert Dossenbach and Oblt Hans Schilling, Fl Abt 22, Cambrai, France, late 1916

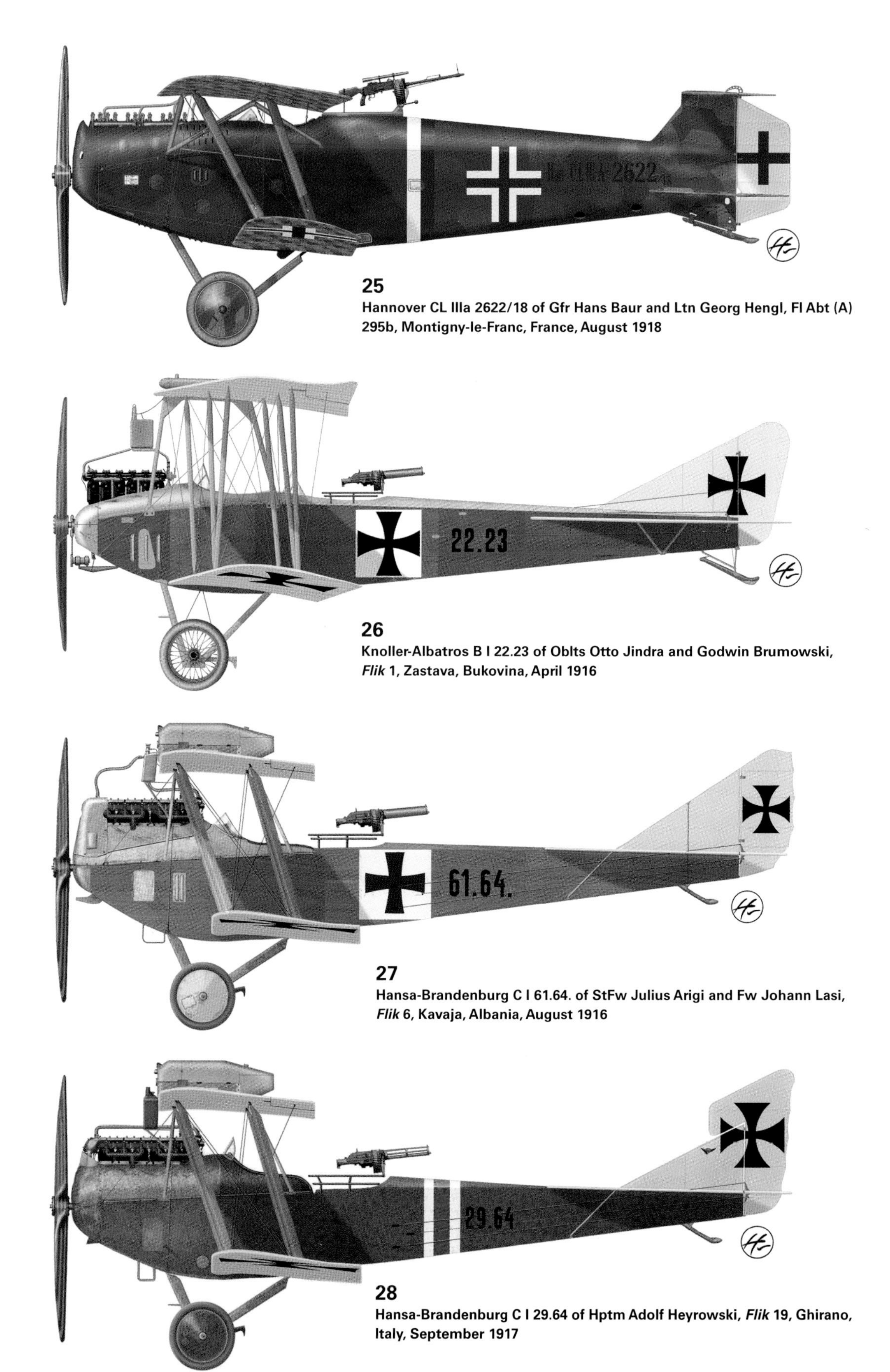

25
Hannover CL IIIa 2622/18 of Gfr Hans Baur and Ltn Georg Hengl, Fl Abt (A) 295b, Montigny-le-Franc, France, August 1918

26
Knoller-Albatros B I 22.23 of Oblts Otto Jindra and Godwin Brumowski, *Flik* 1, Zastava, Bukovina, April 1916

27
Hansa-Brandenburg C I 61.64. of StFw Julius Arigi and Fw Johann Lasi, *Flik* 6, Kavaja, Albania, August 1916

28
Hansa-Brandenburg C I 29.64 of Hptm Adolf Heyrowski, *Flik* 19, Ghirano, Italy, September 1917

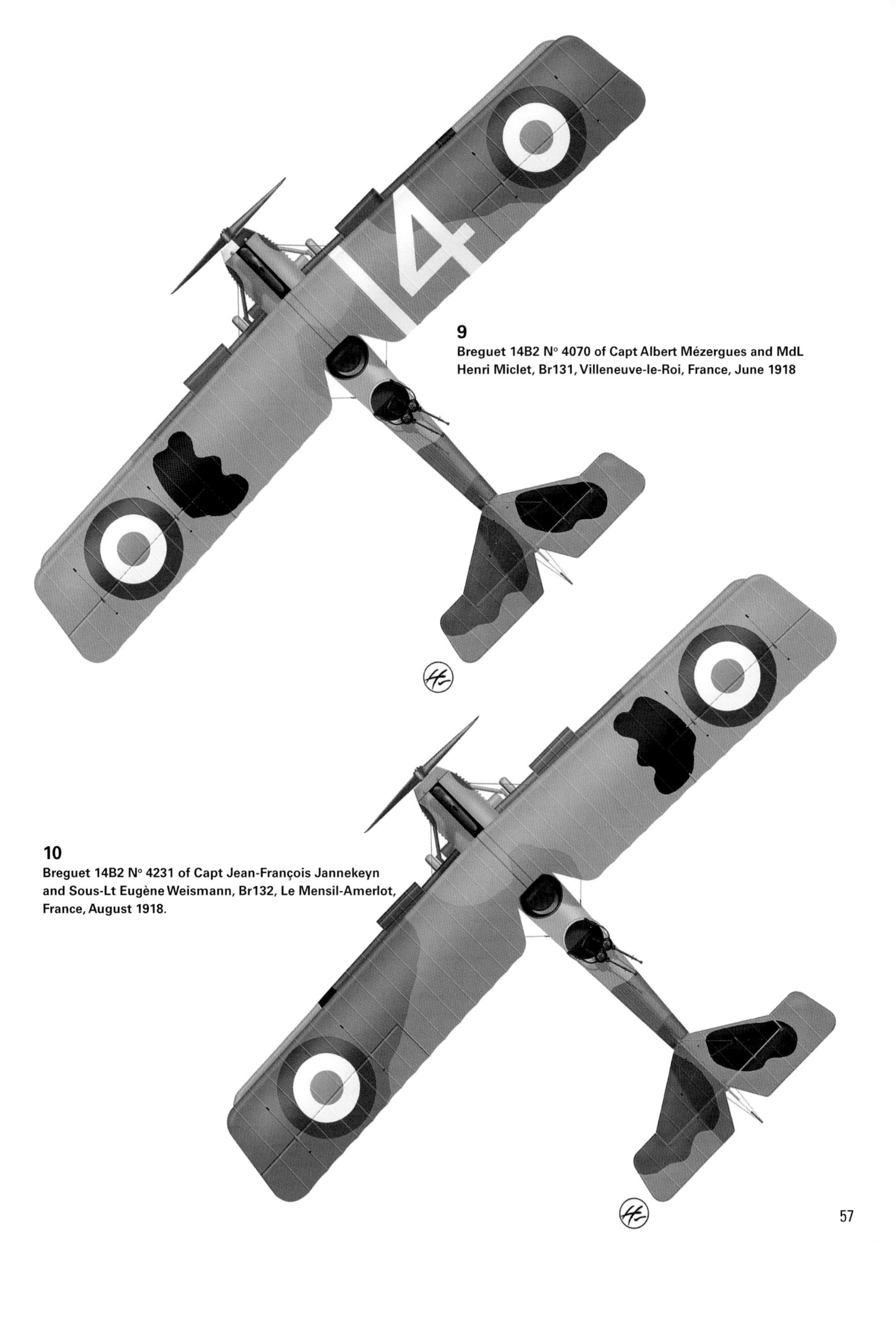

9

Breguet 14B2 N° 4070 of Capt Albert Mézergues and MdL Henri Miclet, Br131, Villeneuve-le-Roi, France, June 1918

10

Breguet 14B2 N° 4231 of Capt Jean-François Jannekeyn and Sous-Lt Eugène Weismann, Br132, Le Mensil-Amerlot, France, August 1918.

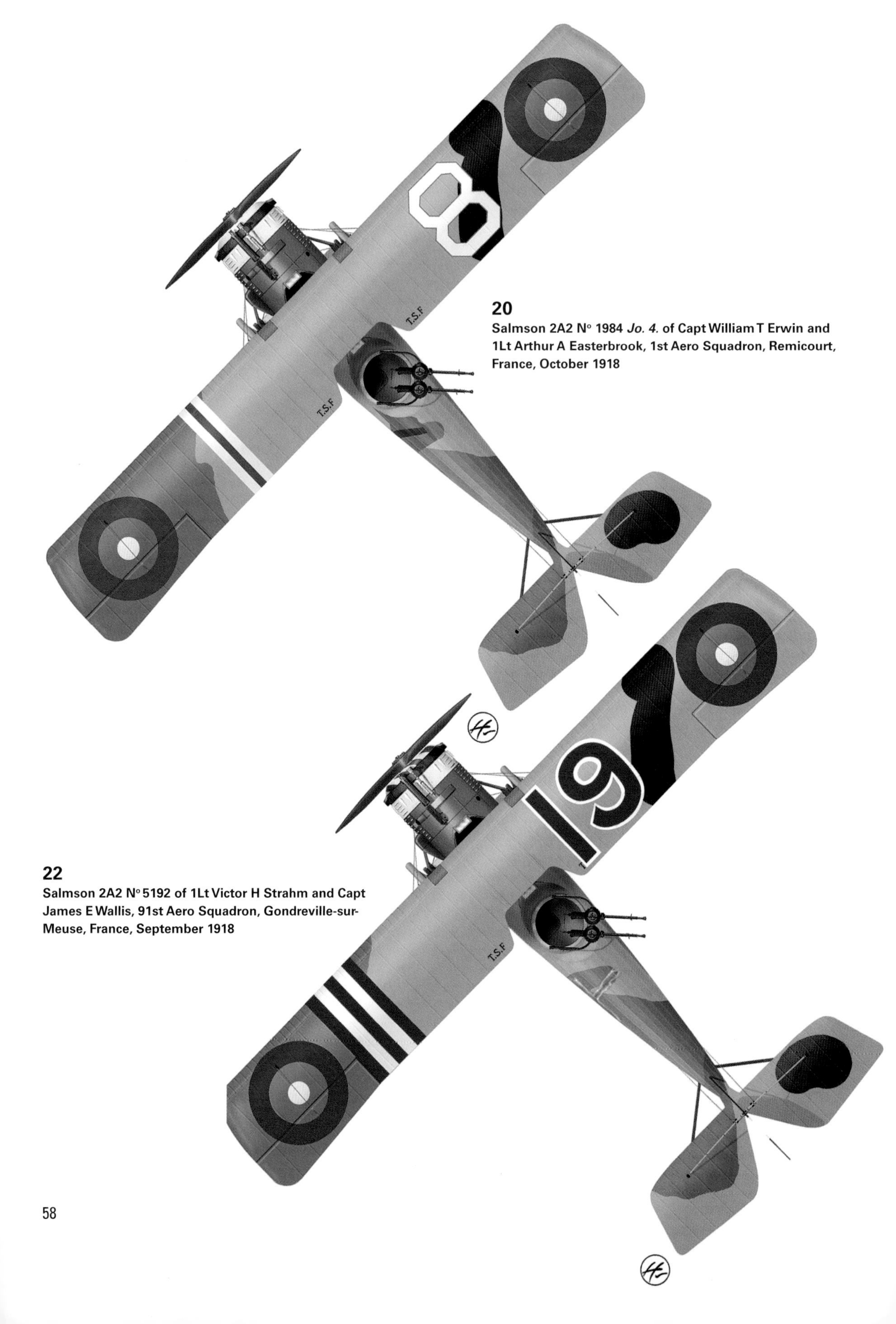

20
Salmson 2A2 N° 1984 *Jo. 4.* of Capt William T Erwin and 1Lt Arthur A Easterbrook, 1st Aero Squadron, Remicourt, France, October 1918

22
Salmson 2A2 N° 5192 of 1Lt Victor H Strahm and Capt James E Wallis, 91st Aero Squadron, Gondreville-sur-Meuse, France, September 1918

Back from a photo mission on 6 August 1918, Maj John N Reynolds switches off the engine of Salmson 2A2 N° 16 of the 91st Aero Squadron while his operations officer, 1Lt John H Snyder, hands over his French 1824-size camera with Berthiot colour lens, which will be despatched by motorcycle to the darkroom for developing (*National Archives*)

GOING DEEP

Although it had not been designed as a two-seat fighter, as was the Bristol F 2B, many Americans flew the Salmson with the same aggressiveness as their 'Biff'-flying colleagues. Three pilots and four observers would achieve acedom in them as a result. Most came from the 91st Aero Squadron, whose missions deep into enemy lines fairly begged for trouble.

2Lt William T Badham's regular pilot during the Saint-Mihiel offensive was 1Lt George C Kenney. On 15 September 1918 they were attacked by three Pfalz, one of which Badham shot down in flames, but Kenney's Salmson, N° 5, was badly shot up and he returned with one elevator almost shot off. Credited with three victories, Kenney went on to command the Fifth Air Force and the Far East Air Force in the South Pacific during World War 2 (*Everett R Cook*)

Based at Gondreville-sur-Moselle, the squadron flew its first operational sortie on 3 June. An early indication of what its men faced occurred on 12 June when 1Lt William A Diekema and 2Lt William T Badham were caught in a barrage of anti-aircraft fire over Arneville that punched 30 holes in their aeroplane, including one in the radiator. Nevertheless, Diekema managed to cross the lines before the engine seized.

Born in Birmingham, Alabama, on 27 September 1895, William Terry Badham had the benefit of previous combat experience.

In April-May 1918 he had been on temporary duty with the French, occupying the observer/gunner's pits of Caudron R 11s with R214, Salmsons with Sal40 and Breguet 14A2s with SAL210.

In the week leading up to the St Mihiel offensive, 1Lt Victor H Strahm was attacked by Pfalz D IIIas on 4 September, but he and his observer, Capt James E Wallis shot one down near Rembercourt, wounding Vfw Alfred Bäder of *Jasta* 65. Victor Herbert Strahm had been born in Nashville, Tennessee, on 26 October 1895, and he had moved to Bowling Green, Kentucky, with his family in 1910 so that his father could head up the music department at Western Kentucky State Normal School (now Western Kentucky University). After graduating from that institution Victor studied engineering at the University of Kentucky. When war broke out he joined the Army in May 1917 and received his commission on 31 October.

On 6 September Maj John N Reynolds passed command of the 91st on to 1Lt E R Cook following his promotion to lead the Army Observation Group. Everett Richard Cook had been born in Indianapolis, Indiana, on 13 December 1894, and he had spent his childhood in Memphis, Tennessee. Cook enlisted in the USAS in May 1917.

The American Expeditionary Force launched its first major offensive at St Mihiel on 12 September. The next day Strahm and Wallis were 25 kilometres behind enemy lines at an altitude of 300 metres when they came under anti-aircraft fire near Metz and were then attacked by fighters, one of which Wallis shot down. The team completed its mission and Strahm was awarded the DSC.

Two future observer aces of the 91st drew attention on 15 September. 'Bill' Badham and his pilot, 1Lt George C Kenney, were credited with a Pfalz D IIIa northwest of Görz, while 1Lts Diekema and Leonard Coombes Hammond fought their way through continuous attacks by enemy fighters, one of which Hammond claimed. It was not confirmed, but he received the DSC for completing his photo-reconnaissance. Born in Missoula, Montana, on 11 November 1884, Hammond was residing in San Francisco, California, when the US entered the war.

On 17 September Cook and 2Lt Alfred W Lawson shot down a Fokker D VII over Crépion. Ten days later Hammond, with 1Lt John W Van Heuvel as his pilot, scored his first official victory when he too downed a Fokker over Crépion. On 10 October Hammond, with Maj Reynolds piloting, downed another D VII over Brieulles. Cook and Badham were credited with a D VII and a Pfalz D IIIa over Andevanne on 23 October, with Badham also returning with 'photographs of great military value', as stated in his DSC citation. That same day 1Lts Kingman Douglass and Hammond fought their way through a Fokker formation, bringing down two.

Cook and Badham shot down a D VII over Malancourt on 28 October and another over Grandpré the next day, taking their tallies to five. Hammond also achieved acedom on the 29th when he and Reynolds were credited with a D VII over Grandpré as well. Two days later Douglass and Hammond, in concert with 2Lts Merle R Husted and William J Moran, despatched a D VII in flames over Damvillers. The 31st also saw two other 91st Salmsons, one crewed by Strahm and 1Lt Thomas M Jervey and the other by 1Lts John H Lambert and John Pope, involved in a running fight with 14 Fokkers over Jametz. Both aeroplanes survived, the crews emerging with two claims to their credit. 'Lambert's ship was pretty well

1Lt Kingman Douglass stands before Capt Victor Strahm's Salmson No 19 at Gondreville-sur-Meuse. Credited with three victories, while his regular observer, 1Lt Leonard Hammond, scored five, Douglass served in Allied intelligence throughout World War 2, retiring from the Central Intelligence Agency in 1952 (*Everett R Cook*)

Observers 1Lts Byrne V Baucom (left) and Arthur E Easterbrook flank William P Erwin, highest scoring Salmson ace of the war. Easterbrook figured in half of 1Lt Erwin's eight victories, while Baucom shared in three of them (*Norman Franks*)

shot up so he turned for home', Merle Husted recalled, 'but even though they had only 100 rounds of ammunition left, Strahm and Jervey finished their mission'.

On 4 November Strahm and Jervey drove down a German two-seater over Conflans – Strahm's fifth victory and Jervey's third. 'I feel that Tom Jervey deserves special recognition amongst the members of the 91st Aero Squadron'. Husted noted. 'He was our ordnance officer, and it was his duty to keep the guns of our ships in tip-top shape. Jervey was neither a pilot nor an observer and had no obligation whatsoever to accompany any of the pilots over the lines. However, due to the shortage of observers at various stages of the game, he decided to go along and do a little looking and a little shooting'.

The 91st Aero Squadron bred a number of career officers for the post-war years. During the 1920s Capt Everett Cook served on Brig Gen William Mitchell's staff, and in World War 2 he was chief of staff for the Eighth Air Force in England, later serving in the Middle East and Europe. Retiring from the USAF Reserve as a brigadier general, he died in Memphis on 21 January 1974. Victor Strahm was involved in aviation research during the 1930s and, like Cook, rose to the rank of brigadier general in the USAAF. On 11 May 1957, however, he reportedly committed suicide in Shreveport, Louisiana.

Of the observers, Leonard Hammond died in San Francisco on 21 December 1945. 'Bill' Badham worked in his father's coal mining business and later formed the Naphthalene Products Company. After retirement he took up painting, and died in Mentone, Alabama, on 6 June 1991, aged 95.

FIRST AMONG SALMSONS

While the 91st produced the most Salmson aces, the leading two-seater ace of the USAS came from the 1st Aero Squadron, a corps observation unit that had seen its debut accompanying Brig Gen John J Pershing's 1916 expedition against Pancho Villa in Mexico. Born in Amarillo, Texas, William Portwood Erwin was living in Chicago, Illinois, when he enlisted. Erwin's DSC citation serves as a reminder that the observation pilot's primary mission was not air-to-air combat;

'Lt Erwin, with Lt Byrne V Baucom, Observer, by a long period of faithful and heroic operations, set an inspiring example of courage and devotion to duty to his entire squadron. Throughout the Château Thierry actions in June and July 1918, he flew under the worst weather conditions and successfully carried out his missions in the face of heavy odds. He flew as low as 50 ft from the ground behind the enemy's lines, harassing German troops with machine gun fire and subjected himself to attack from the ground batteries, machine guns and rifles. He twice drove off enemy

Erwin and Easterbrook return from a sortie in Salmson 2A2 N° 1984 on 1 October 1918. Although this aircraft had only been delivered to the 1st Aero Squadron the day before, it already had bullet holes patched with small crosses and a large hole from a flak hit by the time this photograph was taken. The white stripes below the observer's cockpit were aids for aligning the camera (*US Air Force Museum*)

aeroplanes that were attempting to destroy an American observation balloon. On 12-13 September he flew at extremely low altitudes and carried out infantry contact patrols successfully. Again on 12 September he attacked a German battery, forced the crew to abandon it, shot a German officer who was trying to escape off his horse and drove the cannoneers to their dugouts and kept them there until the infantry could come up and capture them.'

Erwin's first confirmed victory came on 15 September when his observer, 1Lt Homer W Dahringer, shot down an enemy aeroplane over Mamey. Two weeks later he and Baucom downed a Rumpler over Fleville, on 6 October Erwin and 1Lt Arthur Easterbrook were credited with an enemy aeroplane over Saint-Juvin and 48 hours later they despatched a pair of two-seaters. Erwin and Baucom downed a Rumpler on 15 October and a Fokker three days later. Erwin's eighth, and final, success occurred on 22 October when he and Easterbrook shot down a two-seater northwest of Remonville.

Hailing from Amsterdam, New York, Arthur Edmund Easterbrook was serving as a gunnery officer in the 4th Division when he was temporarily assigned to the RAF's No 9 Sqn on 30 May 1918. Having flown 27 missions in RE 8s, he was withdrawn on 19 July and reassigned to the 1st Aero Squadron on 20 August. In addition to his four victories with Erwin, he downed a Fokker D VII with Capt Arthur Coyle as his pilot on 4 November. Easterbrook's conduct during his 8 October mission with Erwin earned him an oak leaf cluster to the DSC he had received on 12 September.

Easterbrook was living in Long Beach, California, when he suffered a bad fall in 1951. He died as a result of his injuries on 24 July 1952.

Born on 19 July 1892, 1Lt Byrne Baucom had seen five weeks of combat as an observer with French Sal5 before joining the 1st Aero

Easterbrook and Capt Arthur J Coyle, with the latter's Salmson N° 24 *Gertrude A*. On 4 November 1918 they were credited with downing a Fokker D VII over Vaux for Coyle's first and Easterbrook's fifth victory (*US Air Force Museum*)

Erwin's third Salmson 2A2 N° 1984, now christened *Jo. 4.* and marked with his victories, after being hit by ground fire and crash landing on 5 November 1918. The aeroplane was not scrapped until after the war, and 'Lone Star' Bill Erwin had already departed the squadron when its much-photographed successor, N° 5464, replaced it *(US Air Force Museum)*

Squadron in mid-July 1918. Credited with as many as seven victories, he certainly accounted for three while occupying Erwin's back seat, on 29 September and 15 and 18 October. Baucom died on 27 May 1927 when his DH 4B crashed near Douglas, Arizona.

'Lone Star' Bill Erwin remained in aviation after the armistice. When pineapple magnate James Dole offered a prize of $25,000 for the first civilian aeroplane to fly nonstop from California to Hawaii, Erwin and navigator Ike Eichwaldt were among those who accepted the challenge. At the same time, however, Dallas broker William Easterwood was offering another $25,000 prize to the first aircrew to fly from Dallas to Hong Kong with no more than three stops, and Erwin aimed to accomplish that feat. From Hong Kong, he planned to circumnavigate the globe.

Dole contestants began taking off from Oakland Municipal Airport on 16 August 1927, but many of the heavily fuelled aircraft failed to leave the ground. Erwin aborted when a tear appeared in the wing fabric of his Swallow monoplane, *Dallas Spirit*. Between crashes, the disappearance of two aircraft at sea and the loss of a US Army Air Corps search aeroplane with its crew, a total of nine men and one woman were killed during the course of the race. The first aeroplane to reach Wheeler Field on Honolulu was the *Woolaroc*, a Travel Air monoplane flown by Arthur C Goebel and William V Davis, after a flight of 26 hours, 17 minutes and 33 seconds. Martin Jensen and Paul Schluter, in a Breese monoplane called *Aloha*, won $10,000 for arriving second.

Erwin, still determined to win the Easterwood Prize, left Oakland on 19 August stating that he intended to search for the two missing contestant aircraft along the way. Eichwaldt reported their progress by radio that night, including a close call involving a spin. Ten minutes later another transmission came from *Dallas Spirit* – 'We are in another . . .'

Nothing more was heard or seen of Erwin or Eichwaldt. Their tragic disappearance brought the Dole Air Race's overall death toll to 12.

GERMAN TWO-SEATER ACES

The German *Inspektion der Fliegertruppen*, or *Idflieg*, had proposed arming aircraft before war broke out. Not until Roland Garros' aerial rampage in April 1915, however, did the Germans launch a serious effort to develop single-seat fighters of their own – most notably the Fokker E I Eindecker – as well as replace their unarmed 'A' class monoplanes and B type biplanes with a new 'C' class of armed two-seaters.

Ironically, the first German warplane to carry a machine gun into battle was the Ago C I pusher, whose 150 hp Benz Bz III engine and aft-spinning propeller were cleared by two streamlined plywood booms supporting the tail surfaces. Armed with a Parabellum LMG 14 in front of the nacelle, at least 64 C Is were built, and they served well into 1916.

The true archetype of the German two-seater, however, came from the Luft-Verkehrs Gesellschaft, whose Swiss-born engineer Franz Schneider had obtained a patent for a series of cams and rods attached to the trigger bar that would interrupt a machine gun's fire whenever the propeller was in its way – the very system that Fokker lifted for his E I! In addition, Schneider had invented an arrangement of concentric rotating rings on which to flexibly mount a Parabellum machine gun, which *Idflieg* had him make available to all other manufacturers. The first German aeroplane to enter service with Schneider's gun mount was the Albatros C I in April 1915.

Schneider's own armed two-seater, the LVG C I, reached frontline units from May 1915. The aeroplane made a name for itself – at least in retrospect – on 4 July, when Ltn Oswald Boelcke and Oblt Heinz von Wühlisch of FFA 62 destroyed a Morane Saulnier L over Valenciennes,

A DFW C V reconnoitres the Western Front in 1917. Introduced at the end of 1916, this product of the Deutsches Flugzeugwerke GmbH typified the general arrangement of most German armed two-seaters. It was a mainstay workhorse of the *Feldflieger Abteilungen* well into 1918 (*Jon Guttman*)

killing Lts Maurice Tétu and Georges *comte* de la Rochefoucault Beauvicourt of MS15. The C I was quickly superseded when the 160 hp Mercedes D III engine became available to power its successor, the C II. With a maximum speed of 81.2 mph (130 kph) and four hours endurance, the LVG C II served as a bomber with *Kampfgeschwader* as well as in the reconnaissance role in *Feldflieger Abteilungen*.

German manufacturers went on to produce an even more varied array of reconnaissance aircraft than the French. Some, like the DFW C V, were versatile workhorses capable of shouldering any task at least competently. In 1917 Rumpler introduced its C IV, the first of a line of long-range photo-reconnaissance aeroplanes built to avoid interception by reaching higher altitudes than most Allied fighters. September 1917 saw the debut of the Halberstadt CL II, soon joined by the Hannover CL II and III – compact, manoeuvrable 'light' two-seaters whose primary mission was close support and ground attack. Equally useful for those roles was the Junkers J I, an all-metal sesquiplane with armoured engine and crew compartments. The German navy had its own variations in floatplane form, from the ubiquitous Friedrichshafen 33 to the Brandenburg W12 biplane and W29 monoplane, which were in essence two-seat fighters on floats.

A Sanke portrait of Ltn Wilhelm Fahlbusch, one of the rare Germans to 'make ace' entirely in two-seaters (*Greg VanWyngarden*)

Relatively few German aircrews attained acedom in two-seaters largely because pilots who showed the requisite aggressiveness were swiftly recommended for fighter training. Among the exceptions were Vfw Willi Fahlbusch and Ltn Hans Rosenkrantz, who gained all of their victories in the sleek, compact, tricky to fly, but fast, Roland C II *Walfisch* ('whale').

Wilhelm Fahlbusch was born in Hanover on 8 February 1892, and after serving in FFA 11 he transferred to a bombing unit, *Kampfstaffel* 1 of *Kampfgeschwader der Obersten der Heeresleitung* (*Kagohl*) 1, on 19 May 1916. There, he and Hans Rosenkrantz, who was born in Wollstein on 6 August 1890, were credited with five victories, although details of only two are known. On 9 July they shot down an RE 7 of No 21 Sqn over Marcoing, killing its Canadian pilot, 2Lt Charles V Hewson. Their fifth success was one of four Martinsyde G100s of No 27 Sqn slaughtered in a disastrous bombing misson to Havricourt Wood on 31 August, the other three falling victim to Halberstadt and Fokker fighters of newly formed *Jasta* 1.

Sharing in 'Willi' Fahlbusch's successes was his observer, Ltn Hans Rosenkrantz. Flying Roland C IIs, the team was credited with five victories before their fatal encounter with a Sopwith 1½ Strutter on 6 September 1916 (*Greg VanWyngarden*)

Both *Walfisch* crewmen were awarded the Iron Cross, but on 6 September American war correspondent Herbert Bayard Swope reported to the *New York Times* that they 'were killed trying to stop an English raiding party of eight aeroplanes that flew over the German lines and were bombarding railroad stations. The flight was at 5.30 Wednesday afternoon and showed the exceptional courage of the Germans in taking on a fight with such superior force'.

Fahlbusch and Rosenkrantz had encountered Sopwith 1½ Strutters of No 70 Sqn over Malincourt. Credit for their deaths was shared between three crews, namely Capt William D S Sanday and Lt Clifford W Busk, Lts Bernard P G Beanlands and C A Good and Lts Selby and Thomas. Sanday, who had scored his first victory in a BE 2c with No 2 Sqn the previous October,

Hptm Konrad Weyert, commander of aircraft for *Heeresgruppe F* in Palestine, and Oblt Franz Walz stand before an LVG C V of Fl Abt 304b in May 1918. Although a seven-victory ace over the Western Front, Walz was awarded the *Orden Pour le Mérite* primarily for his leadership of Fl Abt 304b (*Imperial War Museum M 1259*)

would end up with five victories, while Beanlands added eight more flying DH 5s and SE 5as with No 24 Sqn.

A more famous member of *Kagohl* 1 was ace Franz Josef Walz. Born in Speyer on 4 December 1885, he joined the army on 15 July 1905 and was commissioned in the 8th Bavarian Infantry Regiment in 1908. Learning to fly, he was leading FFA 3 when war broke out. Promoted to oberleutnant in November 1914, Walz was given command of *Kasta* 2 of *Kagohl* 1 on 30 December. He first scored an aerial victory on 9 April 1916 when he downed a Caudron G 4 over Fort Douaumont in concert with observer Ltn Martin Gerlich from neighbouring *Kasta* 4, probably killing Sgt Gaston Guidicelli and Lt Gaston Marchand of C27. Moving to the Flanders front, they drove an RNAS Nieuport into the sea off Dunkirk on 21 May. By July *Kagohl* 1 had been transferred to the Somme area, and the recently promoted Oblt Gerlich had transferred to Walz's *Kasta* 2.

On 3 July Walz and Gerlich were credited with a 'Bristol Scout' south of Péronne, which was in fact BE 2c 5746 of No 16 Sqn flown by a lone New Zealander, 2Lt S H Ellis, who was wounded and taken prisoner. This success was followed by an enemy aeroplane downed west of Neuville on the 9th. Credited with four victories, *'Spatz'* Gerlich became adjutant of *Kagohl* 3 (later redesignated *Bogohl* 3) in August 1917. He survived the war as a hauptmann and became department manager of the Berlin Security Police, but died on 26 February 1920 aged just 27.

On 15 July Walz and an unidentified observer downed Caudron G 4 N° 2149 west of the Somme, killing Cpl André Pichard and Sgt Pierre Tabateau of C106. His sixth victory may have been one of two No 27 Sqn Martinsydes that returned damaged with wounded pilots on 29 July, but the next day he was wounded in the foot. After returning to *Kasta* 2 Walz was awarded the Royal Hohenzollern House Order on 5 September. He was given command of fighter unit *Jasta* 19 on 3 November, switching to *Jasta* 2 on 29 November.

Oblt der Landwehr Josef Neubürger and Vfw Fritz Kosmahl stand before AEG G II 19/15, which after consideration as a 'battle plane' served in the reconnaissance and bombing roles with FFA 22 (*Greg VanWyngarden*)

Although Walz was promoted to hauptmann on 20 January 1917, members of *Jasta* 2 found his leadership so uninspiring that Ltn d R Werner Voss and Ltn Rolf *Freiherr* von Lersner petitioned to have him replaced, pronouncing him 'war weary' and 'no longer fit for service as a *Staffelführer*'. After being reprimanded for skirting the chain of command, Voss was transferred to *Jasta* 5 and von Lersner to *Kagohl* 3. In spite of downing an Airco DH 4 north of Severin Ferme on 14 May, killing six-victory ace Capt William G S Curphey of No 32 Sqn, Walz, believing his leadership compromised, requested reassignment, which finally came with a short-lived command of *Jasta* 34 from 9 to 19 June. He was then shipped off on 25 August to Palestine to command Fl Abt 304b. Resuming the reconnaissance role, he was again able to excel, earning the sobriquet 'The Eagle of Jericho'.

On 22 July 1918 Walz received the Turkish Silver Merit Medal, followed on 9 August by the *Orden Pour le Mérite* – more in recognition of his 500 combat missions than his seven aerial victories. On 20 September he was taken prisoner by the British and held until 1 December 1919.

Walz's post-war service included time in the *Reichswehr* and the State Police. World War 2 found him in the Luftwaffe, attaining the rank of generalleutnant on 1 April 1941. He was captured again, however, this time by the Soviets, and died in captivity in Breslau, Silesia, on 4 December 1945.

Another two-seater pilot who amassed an impressive score before transitioning to fighters was Fritz Gustav August Kosmahl, who was born in Leipzig on 5 September 1892, enlisted in the air service on 12 August 1914 and began training at *Flieger Ersatz Abteilung* (FEA) 2. He joined FFA 22 on 11 January 1915, and was credited with two enemy aircraft in 1916. Kosmahl's third victory, on 10 October, was the subject of a combat report by Ltn Manfred *Freiherr* von Richthofen, then flying Albatros D IIs in *Jasta* 2.

Neubürger and Kosmahl pose with a Roland C II. The duo were credited with four victories, Kosmahl's total ultimately reaching nine, four of which were scored in single-seaters with *Jasta* 26 (*Greg VanWyngarden*)

'At about 1800 hrs I attacked a squad of Vickers at 3500 metres altitude six kilometres in the east of Arras above Roeux. After having singled out a Vickers at whom I fired 300 shots, the enemy aeroplane began to smoke and then started gliding steeper and steeper. I followed, always shooting. The enemy propeller was only going very slowly, and clouds of black smoke were coming from the motor. The observer did not shoot any more at my machine. At this moment I was attacked from the rear.

'As was ascertained later on, the aeroplane crashed to the ground and the occupant was killed.'

Having to break off to deal with a new assailant cost von Richthofen credit for his fifth victory – which was made six days later – but as luck would have it, at that moment Vfw Kosmahl, with Oblt der Landwehr Josef Neubürger in the observer's pit, arrived over Roeux and finished off the 'Vickers', which was actually FE 2b 4292 of No 25 Sqn. The observer, Lt Moreton Hayne, was indeed dead, while the Canadian pilot, 2Lt Arthur H M Copeland, was taken prisoner.

In December FFA 22 was redesignated as artillery-spotting unit Fl Abt (A) 261. While serving with it, recently promoted Offz Stv Kosmahl and Ltn d R Schulz brought down a Sopwith Pup over Hermies on 2 February 1917, killing Flt Lt Walter E Traynor of 8 Naval Squadron. On 11 March Kosmahl, again with Neubürger in the back seat, brought down an FE 2b of No 23 Sqn south of Beugny.

Credited with five victories, Kosmahl underwent fighter training, and in July he joined *Jasta* 26. He opened his account as a *Jagdflieger* on 17 August with an FE 2d of No 20 Sqn over Zonnebeke, and claimed a Camel over Westrozebeke on 9 September – the latter was possibly flown by 2Lt H Wightman of No 70 Sqn, who was wounded in the abdomen but crash landed in Allied lines. Ten days later Kosmahl downed Sopwith Triplane N5490 of 1 Naval Squadron over Passchendaele, Flt Sub-Lt R E McMillan being captured, followed by a Camel 24 hours later.

Ltn Albert Dossenbach poses before Albatros D V/16 C1220/16, which bore an unusual pointed spinner. Just as unusual was the fitting of a captured synchronised Vickers machine gun, rather than an LMG 08/15. Dossenbach and Oblt Hans Schilling flew in this machine but it is not known for certain whether they scored any victories with the aeroplane (*Greg VanWyngarden*)

Kosmahl's luck ran out on 22 September when he was struck in the stomach, his disengagement probably being the Albatros D V 'out of control' jointly credited to SE 5a pilots Capts Robert L Chidlaw-Roberts and Harold A Hamersley of No 60 Sqn. Kosmahl made German lines, but died in hospital at 0230 hrs on the 26th.

Even more successful in two-seaters before making an ill-fated transition to fighters was Albert Dossenbach. Born in the Black Forest town of Blasien on 5 June 1891, Dossenbach had studied medicine and spent time as a hospital intern prior to enlisting following the outbreak of war in August 1914. He soon earned the Iron Cross 2nd Class for carrying his wounded commanding officer to safety under fire. On 27 January 1915 Dossenbach was given a leutnant's commission, and soon after that he transferred into aviation, joining FFA 22 in June 1916. Flying Albatros C IIIs, he was credited with four victories over the next several weeks, two of which were shared with Oblt Hans Schilling.

Born in Zackerick on 24 September 1892, Schilling had observed for FFA 5 before transferring to FFA 22 and scoring his first victory, over a Morane-Saulnier, in the Lille area on 10 January 1916.

On 13 August Dossenbach and Schilling shot down BE 12 6549 of No 19 Sqn near Bapaume, 2Lt G L Clifford-Green being taken prisoner. They claimed another No 19 Sqn BE 12 over Morchies on 24 September, and an unidentified enemy aeroplane two days later. On 27 September Dossenbach and Schilling brought down FE 2b 4839 of No 25 Sqn over Tourmignies, but they were themselves shot down by their victims, Lt V W Harrison and Sgt L S Court, resulting in a crash-landing that left Dossenbach slightly wounded and Schilling slightly burned. On 3 November the duo downed FE 2b 6374 of No 22 Sqn over Mory,

Leutnant Eisenmenger (rechts) und Vfw. Gund,
die bei einem Beobachtungsflug von 6 engl. Kampfeinsitzern
4 Flugzeuge abschossen.
636
Postkartenvertrieb W. Sanke
BERLIN N 37.

Near-aces Ltn d R Karl Eisenmenger and Vfw Georg Gund of Fl Abt (A) 263 were on an artillery shoot in their LVG C V on 23 May 1918 when they were attacked by six British fighters, of which they claimed five and were credited with four, including one in flames. The only possible RAF loss was South African Lt Andries Lars Stockenstrom of No 70 Sqn, who was killed in action that day. Shortly thereafter, Gund was killed in a crash on 9 June and Eisenmenger badly wounded eight days later (*Jon Guttman*)

and on the 11th Dossenbach was awarded the *Orden Pour le Mérite* – the first two-seater pilot to be so honoured.

Soon afterward Schilling teamed up with another pilot, Ltn Rosenbachs. On 4 December, however, the new team perished when their LVG was shot down at Flesquières, west of Nurlu, by Lt Charles Nungesser of N65 for his 19th victory.

On 9 February 1917 Dossenbach was transferred to *Jasta* 2 for fighter training, and he was given command of *Jasta* 36 on the 22nd. He scored the new unit's first official victory (a Caudron) on 5 April, followed by another on the 11th. On 13 April he brought down a SPAD VII whose pilot, Sous-Lt Maurice Nogues of N12, was taken prisoner but later escaped – he fought through to war's end, being credited with 13 victories.

On 15 April Dossenbach scored a 'double' over a Nieuport and a SPAD VII of N15. He was wounded by bomb splinters during an attack on his aerodrome on 2 May, but by 21 June he had recuperated and was given command of *Jasta* 10. Dossenbach burned a balloon at Ypres on the 27th, bringing his total to 15. As he was engaging four DH 4s on 3 July, however, his Albatros caught fire and he fell – or jumped – to his death. Credited to Capt Laurence Minot and Lt A F Brown of No 57 Sqn, Dossenbach was buried in Freiburg.

Besides the single-seat *Jagdstaffeln*, the Germans created 'protection flights' or *Schützstaffeln* in late 1916 to provide two-seater escort for their frontline reconnaissance aeroplanes. At least two aces emerged in the course of these duties.

Rudolf Besel was born in Bronnen on 26 May 1895, and he began the war as a Pionier in the combat engineers. Joining the air service, he initially trained with Bavarian FEA 1 at Schleissheim prior to being assigned to Bavarian *Schützstaffel* 30 at Bisseghem on 17 March 1917.

Uffz Besel's first victory, a Nieuport near Passchendaele on 18 August 1917, has been variously reported as having been scored with either

Schusta 30b observer Ltn F Bayr or Ltn d R Zichäus of Fl Abt (A) 221 – an artillery-spotting unit also based at Bisseghem. On 21 August Besel and Uffz Druschner downed an RE 8 over Ypres, and the next day they were credited with a Sopwith Camel near Frezenberg (a machine from No 70 Sqn was damaged but returned to Allied lines).

Besel and Druschner claimed a British SPAD west of Gheluvelt on 7 October, their opponents from No 19 Sqn, led by Capt Frederick Sowry, reporting that they had attacked an artillery spotter over the lines but were driven off by a large formation of fighters, suffering no actual loss.

On 16 October Besel got another promotion, to vizefeldwebel. He and Druschner struck again on 4 December, downing a Bristol Fighter over Bellwalde Lake. Bristol F 2B B1153 of No 22 Sqn came down near Ypres, and its crew, 2Lts A G F Goodchap and A H Middleton, were captured.

On 27 March 1918 Besel was withdrawn to *Armee-Flugpark* 2 and on 17 April he returned to FEA 1b at Schleissheim as an instructor. He also undertook test flying at the Rumpler factory in Augsburg and with Zeppelin at Lindau. On 23 August he was transferred to the *Militär-Fliegerschule* at Gerstofen, but on 7 September 1918, during a hop with trainee pilot Pionier Franz Egger, their Albatros C X crashed and both men were killed.

Less is known of Oswald Tränker, an observer in *Schusta* 16. Uffz Walter Reichenbach was his pilot on 7 May 1917 when they were credited with a Nieuport near Pontavert and a Caudron over La Ville-aux-Bois. Three days later Reichenbach, born in Ribnitz on 19 January 1890, was also credited with a SPAD over Berry-au-Bac, with Flg Misiak as his observer. Reichenbach subsequently transferred to *Jasta* 5. On 25 July, however, his Albatros scout crashed near Busigny and he died of his injuries that same day.

In June 1917 *Schusta* 16 moved to Ichtegem, in Flanders, and on 7 July Tränker, with Fw Haefer as his pilot, shot down a Sopwith over Mannekensvere. This may have been a Pup from 9 Naval Squadron, which crashed in Allied lines after a combat – its pilot, Flt Sub-Lt J C Tanner, died of his injuries. Promoted to vizefeldwebel that same month, Tränker again teamed up with Haefer to down Pup N6460 near Oostkerke on 3 September. The pilot, Flt Sub-Lt N D Hall of 3 Naval Squadron, was captured. Tränker had Vfw Schneider as his pilot on 24 January 1918 when they shared in bringing down a DH 4, possibly from No 57 Sqn, near Méricourt. Nothing further is known of Tränker's whereabouts, save that he survived the war.

Since mid-1917 the *Schützstaffeln* had played a growing close support role with the Halberstadt and Hannover aircraft they had acquired. That was reflected in the decision to redesignate them as *Schlachtstaffeln* (battle flights) in late March 1918. One such unit, *Schlasta* 15, would produce the most successful German two-seater crew of the war.

The observer, Flg Gottfried Ehmann, first joined *Schusta* 15 and 'rode into battle' aboard a Halberstadt CL II, with Flgmr Warda as his pilot, to bring down a SPAD over Fort Douaumont on 30 October 1917. On 21 March 1918 the Germans launched their great Western Front offensive, with a thick morning fog aiding their ground forces but restricting air activity until midday. Once the weather improved the *Schlachtstaffeln*, including the redesignated *Schlasta* 15, fell upon the Allied defences –

Fw Friedrich Huffzky and Uffz Gottfried Ehmann pose in the cockpit of their Halberstadt CL II of *Schlasta* 15 in 1918 (*Greg VanWyngarden*)

amid which Warda and Ehmann were credited with a Sopwith. After bringing down an Armstrong-Whitworth FK 8 north of Cachy on 24 April, both men were awarded the Iron Cross 2nd Class and promoted to gefreiter and unteroffizier, respectively.

It was at this point that Ehmann was assigned a new pilot, Fw Friedrich Huffzky, and the two got off to a good start on 4 June with an AR 2 downed northeast of Villers-Bretonneux, followed by an RE 8 on 25 June. Amid generally cloudy weather on 5 July they were credited with a Sopwith Dolphin south of Hamel. Curiously, however, the only comparable British record attributed a two-seater 'driven down' by, but not credited to, Lt Richard A Hewitt of No 87 Sqn, suggesting a curious case of mutual misperception.

The Second Battle of the Marne put Huffzky and Ehmann through a welter of activity. They downed two SPADs on 18 July, a SPAD XI and a second SPAD on the 21st, a French two-seater on the 24th and a Sopwith on the 29th. This last success brought Huffzky's total to nine victories and Ehmann's to 12, along with two unconfirmed. In curious contrast to their fighter pilot contemporaries, nothing more is known about these workhorse aces.

Although Hannovers also served with distinction in the *Schlachtstaffeln*, the only aces to fly one were attached to a Bavarian artillery-spotting unit. Born near Mühldorf on 24 April 1897, Gfr Hans Baur was assigned to Fl Abt (A) 295b at Montigny-le-Franc, usually flying with Ltn Georg Hengl as his observer during the course of his 160 missions.

Hengl, born in Laiding, Lower Bavaria, in October 1897, had enlisted in 1914 and seen service in the infantry near Ypres, then in Russia, Serbia and Verdun, where he was commissioned on 23 March 1916. After further service in Russia, Hengl commenced observer training on 23 February 1918 and was subsequently posted to Fl Abt (A) 295b.

During the Battle of the Aisne, Baur and Hengl were brought down and captured by the British, although they were subsequently rescued by soldiers of a Württemberg regiment. In a scrap with seven SPADs over the Forêt de Courton on 17 July Baur and Hengl downed two and forced two others to land in their own lines. This engagement was apparently fought with SPA103, which in turn claimed two probable victories over Cuchery and Jonchery but lost Adj Auguste Baux, the five-victory ace being shot down and killed by a two-seater near Cuchery.

Uffz Baur and Hengl were credited with a Breguet and another French aeroplane over Barricourt on 22 August. Hengl downed a French machine while with another pilot on 5 October, but on 29 October he and Bauer reunited to shoot down two SPADs of SPA163, killing MdL Jean Antoine and wounding Sgt Paul Lefebvre. Two subsequent SPAD claims went unconfirmed.

Hengl, who also received the Max Josef Award that elevated him to knighthood as Georg *Ritter* von Hengl, enlisted in the *Gebirgsjäger* in 1935 and during World War 2 rose to general in command of a corps and received the Knight's Cross of the Iron Cross. An Allied prisoner until 1947, he died in Sonthofen on 19 March 1952.

A vizefeldwebel at war's end, 'Hans' Baur gained his greatest notoriety in the 1930s as Adolf Hitler's personal pilot, flying Junkers Ju 52/3ms and Focke-Wulf Fw 200s and attaining the rank of SS-oberstgruppenführer (the SS equivalent of an army generaloberst). After the war the Soviets imprisoned him in Siberia for ten years, during which time he had to have a gangrenous leg amputated by a dental technician using locally brewed vodka as an anaesthetic. Baur survived his harsh captivity to be released in 1955 and lived to the age of 95, dying in Munich on 17 February 1993.

Ltn Georg Hengl and Vfw Hans Baur beside Hannover CL IIIa 2522/18 at Montigny-le-Franc aerodrome on 20 August 1918. They had claimed a victory that day, although it was not confirmed. The two French aeroplanes they shot down 48 hours later would be, however. Of note is the telescopic sight mounted on the observer's stripped-down Parabellum MG 14 machine gun (*Greg VanWyngarden*)

DEADLY DUOS OF THE DUAL MONARCHY

With the benefit of hindsight, Austria-Hungary's declaration of war on Serbia, which ignited the worldwide conflagration, seems all the more ironic when one considers that the Dual Monarchy was among the most backward of the European powers. This is most telling in regard to its aviation industry, which produced about 5000 aeroplanes and 4000 engines during the war, compared to 20,000 airframes and 38,000 engines built in Italy. At any peak period the Austro-Hungarians had just 500 aeroplanes to cover the Russian, Balkan and Italian fronts.

None too astonishingly the *kaiserliche und königliche Luftfahrtruppen* (kuk LFT) generally lagged behind its German allies in aircraft development as well, although it came to produce some robust and reliable reconnaissance two-seaters. It may be noted, however, that some of their best early designs, such as the Knoller-Albatros B II and the

Zgf Julius Arigi poses with a Lohner B VII, with the pilot's seat forward and a rear-mounted Schwarzlose M 7/12 machine gun for the observer. It was in *Pfeil* 17.19 that Arigi was brought down and captured by the Montenegrins on 14 October 1915, although he eventually escaped (*via Aaron Weaver*)

Zgf Julius Arigi sits in the rear (pilot's) seat of Lohner B II C 11 of *Flik* 6 at Igalo, in Dalmatia, in the summer of 1915. Noteworthy are the swept-back wings that earned this series the popular sobriquet of *Pfeil* (arrow). Arigi's hand rests on a primitive machine gun mount (*via Aaron Weaver*)

ubiquitous Hansa-Brandenburg C I, were German. The latter, designed by Ernst Heinkel, offered a combination of creditable performance, ruggedness and close proximity of observer and pilot. That, combined with the skill and courage of its crews, yielded a remarkable number of ace teams at a time when the LFT had no fighters to escort them – the first few that entered combat in February 1916 were imported Fokker E Is, designated A IIIs by the Austrians.

As with the Germans, a good many Austro-Hungarian aces opened their accounts in two-seaters and went on to complete their scoring in single-seaters. An exceptional handful claimed five or more victories solely in two-seaters, including the only Austro-Hungarians credited with five in a single combat that was both celebrated and controversial. The pilot involved in this action, Julius Arigi, was born in Tetschen, in the Sudetenland (now Děčín in the Czech Republic) on 3 October 1895. Joining the artillery on 5 October 1913, he transferred to the Airship Section and gained his pilot's certification on 23 November 1914 as a zugsführer. Assigned to *Fliegerkompagnie* (Flik) 6 at Igalo, in Dalmatia, he was forced by engine trouble to land in Montenegrin lines in October 1915. After several failed attempts Arigi escaped with five fellow prisoners in January 1916 and drove them through the lines in a Fiat touring car that he had stolen from Prince Nikolaus of Montenegro!

August 1916 found *Flik* 6 at Kavaja, southwest of Tiranë, now the capital of Albania. On the 22nd of that month Arigi's section leader, Oblt Emil Cioll, learned that six Italian Farmans were en route to bomb the port of Durazzo. Arigi's request for permission to intercept them was repeatedly denied because there were no officers on the field to man the rear machine gun, and the hidebound LFT – in contrast to the German

Luftstreitskräfte – would not allow enlisted pilots up without an officer-observer's supervision. After two more frustrated entreaties the approaching Italians' engines became audible and Arigi, throwing caution to the wind, took off with Fw Johann Lasi, a 25-year-old Croatian mechanic who had flown 14 bombing missions, manning the rear gun.

A cartwright before the war, whom fate momentarily placed in an officer's position, StFw Johann Lasi wears (from left) the Silver Bravery Medal, First Class, the Silver Merit Cross with Crown and the 1912-13 Commemoration Cross (*via Aaron Weaver*)

The Farmans of *34ª Squadriglia* were first intercepted between Cape Laghi and the Skumbi River Estuary by Lohner Type TI flying boat L131, crewed by Frglt Friedrich Lang and Einjährig-Freiwilliger Stabsmachinenwärter Franz Kohlhauser, who caused them to jettison their bombs and claimed to have driven two down into the water. By then Arigi and Lasi had caught up with the formation, and over the next 30 minutes they claimed to have downed five at the mouth of the Skumbi River. The Italians only recorded two aeroplanes lost, with any others (and their crews) being recovered by destroyers and restored to service. One man, Capt Franco Scarioni, was wounded.

After Arigi and Lasi returned to Kavaja, Oblt Cioll received three telegrams from his superiors in Vienna, not to congratulate the duo on their unprecedented achievement but demanding to know why there had been no officer-observer in the victorious aircraft. Cioll's final response was a sheepish 'All of our officers were indisposed at the time'.

At the end of August 1916 Lasi underwent flight training. From June 1917 to the end of the war he served as a flight instructor at *Fliegerersatzkompagnie* (*Flek*) 1.

Arigi scored twice more in his Brandenburg C I in September, and at the end of the year he was transferred to the Isonzo Front. Flying Brandenburg D I fighters with *Fluggeschwader* I, Oeffag-Albatros D IIIs in *Flik* 55/J and Österreichisches Aviatik (Berg) D Is in *Fliks* 6/F and 1/J, he brought his total to 32, making him Austria-Hungary's second-ranking ace. During World War 2 Arigi served as a fighter instructor in the Luftwaffe, eventually passing away in Attersee, Austria, on 1 August 1981.

A curious phenomenon unique to World War 1 was the view taken by senior military officers that personnel no longer deemed fit for service in the trenches could prove useful in aviation. One such individual was Otto Jäger, who was serving as a fähnrich in der Reserve with the 67th Infantry Regiment in Russia when he was wounded on 30 August 1914, struck in the chest on 21 March 1915 and hit in the lung on 17 May. At that point he was pronounced unfit for the infantry and made a training officer in Hungary. Finding the inactivity unacceptable, he applied for the LFT and was accepted for training at Wiener-Neustadt as an observer and technical officer.

Soon after being assigned to *Flik* 10 in Russia, Ltn d R Jäger was flying in Knoller-Albatros B I 22.10 with the unit's best pilot, Zgf Karl Urban, on 5 May 1916 when they reported encountering a 'large battle plane' over Kol Noviny. In the ensuing chase Jäger expended 300 rounds before his gun jammed. Urban then started firing at the aeroplane with his carbine until Jäger cleared his jam, and after another 25 minutes of fighting the big Russian machine turned around and force landed on its own side of the lines. Infantry witnesses confirmed Jäger's and Urban's

Ltn d R Otto Jäger served with *Flik* 10 in Russia in late 1916. A Sudeten German born in Asch, West Bohemia, he had attended the State Trade School but joined the army in 1909. Thrice wounded and declared unfit for the infantry, he relinquished training duties for a return to action in the air (*Muzeum Cheb via Zdenek Cejka*)

first victory, which seems to have been a four-engined Sikorsky Il'ya Muromets, although it was clearly not a total loss to the Russians.

On 3 June Jäger and Zgf Fritz Rottmann, along with another Albatros crew, forced a 'large Farman' to land and on the 7th Urban and Jäger, again in 22.10, similarly forced two Farmans to make emergency landings. On 2 August, flying Brandenburg C I 64.15, they engaged another Farman which, after Jäger had fired 100 rounds, crashed in a wood, killing its crew. After further two-seater assignments, Urban flew Phönix D Is with *Flik* 14/J, scoring a fifth victory over a Hanriot on 19 May 1918. While test flying experimental Phönix fighter 20.22 on 12 July, however, the wing structure failed and Urban crashed to his death.

Jäger was promoted to oberleutnant on 1 August 1916 and, in September, withdrawn for flight training. From mid-March 1917 he flew successively with *Fliks* 17, 3 and 27. Flying a new Oeffag-Albatros D III in the last unit, he intercepted a Russian two-seater 'with a stationary engine' near Wybudow (now Vybudiv, Ukraine) and forced it to make an emergency landing – the first victory for the Austrian-built version of the German sesquiplane fighter.

In early August Jäger was posted to *Flik* 42/J at Sesana, on the Isonzo Front, and on the 19th he and Fw Vinzenz Magerl claimed an Italian two-seater over Monte Ermada – in actuality the Savoia-Pomilio SP 2 they attacked made it back to base. Magerl was then shot up by a SPAD VII flown by Tenente Alberto Marazzani of *77ª Squadriglia*. As Jäger climbed to his wingman's aid, he was jumped by Marazzani's squadronmate, Tenente Giovanni De Briganti. Moments later his new Albatros 153.14 shed a wing and he fatally crashed near Ivanograd.

Austria's most successful two-seater pilot, Adolf Heyrowsky, was born in Murau, Styria, on 18 February 1882. The son of a gamekeeper, he graduated from the Infantry Military Academy in Prague in 1902 and had attained the rank of oberleutnant by 1910. In 1912 he volunteered for the airship service, quickly qualifying for his pilot's badge and also participating in army manoeuvres as an observer. Besides proving himself a natural aviator, Heyrowsky was also adept at fencing, skiing, swimming, horse riding, automobile driving and motor mechanics.

The outbreak of war found Heyrowsky in *Flik* 2, supporting Austria-Hungary's invasion of Serbia with six elderly Lohner *Pfeil* biplanes. Operating as far as 125 miles over the rough Balkan terrain, he submitted reports that contributed to such successes as his army achieved amid a generally unsuccessful campaign.

By 13 September the Austro-Hungarians had been thrown back to the border and the Serbian Timok Division was building a pontoon bridge across the Sava River in an attempt to invade Syrmia and outflank the enemy. After spotting this activity, Heyrowsky and Rittm Stefan *Frhr* von Ankershofen attacked the bridge using the only bombs available. Lighting the timed fuses to the bombs cradled in his arms and steering the aeroplane with his knees, Heyrowsky dived, timing his descent until at an altitude of 600 ft he threw the bombs down on the bridge, one after the other. Remarkably, they struck the target, destroying the centre span and stalling the Serbian advance until an Austro-Hungarian counterattack wiped out most of the Timok Division.

In mid-November Heyrowsky was given command of *Flik* 9, and he celebrated the New Year with a promotion to hauptmann. On 22 February 1915 he and Oblt Oskar Safar destroyed a Serbian observation balloon near Belgrade, and burned another on 3 March. In August Heyrowsky was transferred to the Isonzo Front as commander of *Flik* 12. In January 1916 he took command of another newly forming unit, *Flik* 19, at Haidenschaft in the Wippach Valley. An able administrator and strict but fair disciplinarian who led by example, Heyrowsky turned *Flik* 19 into the LFT's premier reconnaissance squadron, six of his pilots going on to become aces. One, Oblt d R Benno Fiala, *Ritter* von Fernbrugg, was his observer in Brandenburg C I 61.55 when they encountered Italian airship M4 over Merna on 4 May. One of their machine guns was loaded with 8 mm Alder 'B' explosive anti-balloon ammunition, and after firing 53 rounds they saw M4 fall in flames – Commandante Giovanni Pastine and his five crewmen all perished. This was Heyrowsky's third and Fiala's second victory.

On 6 August the Italians launched another Isonzo offensive. Three days later Heyrowsky, in C I 61.61, was attacked by a Voisin, five Caudrons

After taking command of *Flik* 19, Hptm Adolf Heyrowsky alternated between flying reconnaissance missions and leading an infantry company on the ground during the Fifth Battle of the Isonzo from 9 to 18 March 1916 (*via Aaron Weaver*)

Aspirante Alessandro Resch of *26ª Squadriglia* checks out the controls of his SIT-built Voisin 3 while his observer takes aboard a 162 mm bomb. During a bombing raid on the railway station at Reifenberg (now Branik, in Slovenia), Resch was attacked by two Fokker A IIIs, and he and his observer, Sottotenente Vincenzo Lioy, claimed one of them. The Austro-Hungarians, however, recorded the deaths of both fighter pilots. It was the first of five victories for Resch, the only Italian ace to score his first success in a two-seat bomber (*Roberto Gentilli*)

When he transferred from *Flik* 19 to *Flik* 51/J in October 1917, István Fejes had five two-seater victories and credentials that read in part, 'An earnest, modest, industrious and dependable flier. Speaks bad German. Good technical knowledge'. He would add 11 more to his tally flying Oeffag Albatros D IIIs (*via Aaron Weaver*)

and three Nieuports. After a 45-minute fight he force-landed in Austrian lines. The aeroplane was hastily repaired, and Heyrowsky was flying it on 10 August when he was again attacked over Gorizia by a 'Voisin' and two Nieuports. He and his observer, Oblt Ferdinand Lerch, were credited with downing the Voisin near Cormons, but he had to force land his own riddled aeroplane at the Austrian airfield at Aisovizza. Italian records stated that a Farman of *45ª Squadriglia, 2º Gruppo di Ricognizione* returned with flak damage, its crew, Sottotenente V Bonomi and Capitano F Mattioli, being unhurt.

On 15 August Heyrowsky, flying Fokker A III 03.42, brought down another Voisin for his only single-seater success. He was duly chased back to his aerodrome by three vengeful Nieuports. Again, Italian records mention no loss, but on the same day two other Fokkers fell victim to a Voisin of *26ª Squadriglia* crewed by Aspirante Alessandro Resch and Sottotenente Vincenzo Lioy, killing Fw István Szücs of *Flik* 19 and Fw Franz Gregl of *Flik* 28. One of them was confirmed as the Italians' first victory, to which Resch would later add four more as a fighter pilot.

On 3 December Heyrowsky and Fähnrich Stefan Wagner, together with Fw Heinrich Mahner and his observer, future ace Ltn Sandor Tahy, caught a Caproni bomber returning from a raid on Trieste and forced it down in Italian lines near Gorizia. On the 28th Heyrowsky and Ltn d R Josef Pürer downed a Voisin west of San Marco Argentano.

In mid-March 1917 *Flik* 19 was assigned to support the 14th Infantry Division. On 14 April Heyrowsky was flying C I 29.64, with Pürer again his observer, when they were attacked by a Nieuport. Heyrowsky was wounded in the right eye, but he and Pürer, together with Zgf István Fejes and Oblt Oskar Zeisberger, sent the Nieuport down to crash between the Gorizia train station and the road to Salcano.

On 12 May the Tenth Battle of the Isonzo began, and three days later Heyrowsky, back in 29.64 with Oblt Ladislaus Hauser in the observer's pit, downed a SPAD in Italian territory near Merna. On 3 June he and Hauser, again in 29.64, shared in the destruction of a Nieuport at Sober with two other teams – Zgf Karl Reithofe and Ltn Pürer, and Korp János Szeikovics and Ltn Tahy. Heyrowsky and Hauser were effective in 29.64 once again on 26 June when they shot down a Nieuport and a Caudron over Sober. These were Heyrowsky's last victories. During the Twelfth Battle of the Isonzo, better known as Caporetto, he and Hauser were shot down by ground fire in C I 129.60, but amid the confusion of the Italian rout they were able to make their way back to Austro-Hungarian territory on foot after two days of evading possible capture.

Ltn Sandor Tahy while serving in *Flik* 19 at Haidenschaft on the Isonzo Front in 1917. He wears the Silver Bravery Medal First Class for Officers (*via Aaron Weaver*)

Jindrich Kostrba ze Skalice as deputy commander of *Flik* 4 in the cockpit of Fokker A III 03.52 at Haidenschaft aerodrome in February 1916. Oblt d R Ludwig Hautzmayer shot down a Caproni Ca 1 in this aeroplane on 18 February – his first of seven victories, three in fighters. Kostrba, credited with three flying 03.51 that same day, became an ace in two-seaters thereafter (*via Aaron Weaver*)

For his overall performance Heyrowsky was awarded the Order of Leopold with War Decoration and Swords, and also made air staff officer for the Second Isonzo Army. In March 1918 he was appointed liaison officer to Generalleutnant Ernst Wilhelm von Hoeppner, commander of the German *Luftstreitskräfte*. While visiting the Western Front, he participated in bombing missions with *Bogohl* 6 and 2 to Nancy, Amiens and Paris, and even raided Dover in a Zeppelin Staaken of *Riesenflugzeug Abteilung* 500.

Rushing back from Germany to fight in the last Austro-Hungarian offensive over the Piave between 15 and 25 June 1918, Heyrowsky tried to coordinate air and ground operations. After the failure of the offensive he returned to Germany, where he was when the war ended.

During World War 2 Heyrowsky entered Luftwaffe service as an oberst, and he subsequently died on 4 April 1945 just as he was about to be promoted to generalmajor.

As mentioned earlier, *Flik* 19 bred six other aces. Although Benno Fiala, *Ritter* von Fernbrugg (28 victories), Franz Rudorffer (11) and Ludwig Hautzmeyer (7) did most of their scoring later in fighters, three pilots claimed at least five victories in Brandenburg C Is.

Born in Nyiregyháza in 1896, Sandor Tahy had earned the Silver Bravery Medal in the heavy artillery before attending Officers' Flight School at Wiener-Neustadt between July and September 1916 and qualifying as an observer. While in *Flik* 12 at Haidenschaft he got into an altercation with his commander, Hptm Arpád Gruber, that was resolved only when Hptm Heyrowsky offered Tahy a post in his nearby unit. On 3

Typifying the mounts of so many Austro-Hungarian two-seater aces, Hansa-Brandenburg C I 26.09 was assigned to *Flik* 23 and crewed by Hptm Kostrba and Oblt János Frint when they forced down an Italian two-seater on 9 June 1916 and drove down three Farmans 20 days later (*Colin Owers*)

December Tahy, with Fw Franz Mahner as his pilot, helped Heyrowsky and Wagner down a Caproni, although Tahy was slightly wounded. On 11 May 1917 Korp Ernst Heinz and Tahy, along with two other Brandenburg crews, downed a Nieuport.

On 14 May Tahy had fellow Hungarian Zgf István Fejes as his pilot when they destroyed a Nieuport near Merna, probably killing Tenente Francesco Brioili of *76ª Squadriglia*. Born in Gyömöre on 30 August 1891, Fejes had been in the infantry until wounded on 16 September 1914, subsequently serving in the Motor Service and then the LFT. On 3 February 1917 Fejes reported to *Flik* 19, and on 17 April he and his observer, Oblt Oskar Zeisberger, claimed a Nieuport in concert with Heyrowsky and Pürer. On 3 June another Nieuport fell to Szeikovicz and Tahy, Heyrowsky and Hauser and Reihofer and Pürer. When Fejes and Tahy shared in an Italian Caudron's demise with Heyrowsky and Hauser, it was victory number five for both men.

In July *Flik* 51/J was organised at Haidenschaft, and Fejes was transferred to the unit in October. Tahy also asked to be trained to fly fighters and *Flik* 51/J's commander, Rittm Wedige von Froreich, approved his request. Subsequently flying Oeffag-Albatros D IIIs with the unit, Tahy had added three more victories to his tally by 21 February 1918 and was promoted to oberleutnant. While flying over Mansue on 7 March, however, Tahy's Albatros D III 153.69 suddenly fell into a fatal spin, possibly due to wing failure.

Another observer who made an even shorter-lived transition to fighters was Josef Pürer. Born in Schönau on 20 October 1894. He was credited with six victories as observer to Heyrowsky and Fejes, among others. Pürer qualified as a pilot in 1918 and returned to the front flying Albatros D IIIs with *Flik* 3/J at Romagnano. On 31 August he and three equally inexperienced colleagues lost track of their flight leader, Oblt Franz Peter, and came under attack over Monte Campomolon by RAF Sopwith Camels of No 45 Sqn. In minutes Ltn d R Stanislav von Tomicki and Ltn d R Jaroslav Kubelik were killed by Lt Mansell R James, while Stabsfw Otto Förster and Lt d R Pürer were slain by Lt Jack Cottle. Upon seeing Pürer's identity card, Cottle thought he bore such a disturbing resemblance to a favourite cousin in the Tank Corps who had recently been killed that he requested, and received, immediate leave.

Unlike most of his contemporaries, Fejes survived the war (as a stabsfeldwebel) with 16 victories to his name. In 1919 he flew Fokker D VIIs in the 8th Squadron of Hungary's Red Air Force until May, when he was forced down at Losonc with a damaged propeller and captured by Czechoslovakian troops. He was subsequently involved in the clandestine training of Hungarian military pilots at Szombathely, flew commercial aircraft for MALERT and was a military transport and command liaison pilot during World War 2. Fejes died in Budapest on 1 May 1951.

Arguably the starkest exception to the aces' rule was one of the first Austro-Hungarians to score victories in single-seat fighters, but who then achieved acedom after reverting to two-seaters. Born in Prague in 1883, Jindrich (Heinrich) Kostrba ze Skalice had initially served in the infantry from 1903 before becoming an observer prewar. His performance with *Flik* 8 on the Russian front earned him promotion to hauptmann in May 1915.

Italy's declaration of war led to *Flik* 8's transfer to that sector, and in July Kostrba's request for flight training was approved. He received his Austrian certificate on 29 October 1915, and in December was assigned to *Flik* 4 at Haidenschaft. While flying one of the first Fokker A IIIs to arrive Kostbra was credited with bringing down three Caproni Ca 1 bombers on 18 February 1916. In March he was appointed commander of *Flik* 23 on the southern Tyrolean front, where he scored his next five victories in two-seaters. His observer in four of them was Oblt János Frint.

Kostrba described his Hungarian teammate János Frint as 'a quiet, resolute and clear-sighted man, inspired by the best sense of duty'. Although a highly decorated observer ace, Frint was destined to have a less auspicious pilot's career (*via Aaron Weaver*)

Born in Budapest on 6 May 1888, Frint was a skilled horseman, cyclist, motorist and swimmer. After being wounded in Russia on 14 November 1914 he was judged unfit for infantry service, but entered the LFT as an observer with *Flik* 23. On 16 April 1916 he and Korp Ernst Kerschischnig, in Lloyd C III 43.60, drove a Farman down in Italian territory. On 7 June Kostrba and Frint, in Brandenburg C I 26.09, had a spirited fight with a Farman whose Italian crew matched their skill and aggressiveness. Frint, manning a captured Italian Fiat-Revelli gun, fired more than 500 rounds before the Farman finally force landed and flipped over in a meadow near Corno d'Aquilio. On 29 June Kostrba and Frint took on a large enemy formation over Monte Pasubio for 65 minutes and were credited with a 'large Farman' as well as two smaller ones. Intercepted enemy transmissions identified two Italian crewmen killed and two wounded.

Frint was with Zgf Ernst Franz in C I 26.15 on 4 August when they were attacked by four Italian scouts. Frint, firing 150 rounds, drove a Nieuport down to force land near Val Grazzana, then photographed it with his camera.

The following month Frint began flight training but he proved to be a mediocre pilot, possibly due to his earlier war wound. The LFT limited him to various training units until September 1917, when he was finally put in command of *Flik* 27. On 25 February 1918 he was test flying Albatros D III 53.46 when one of its wings failed and the aeroplane crashed in an orchard near Auer aerodrome, killing Frint.

On 20 August 1916 Kostrba, flying 26.09 without an observer, drove a Farman down in Italian lines for his eighth victory. In November 1916 he was transferred to command *Flik* 2. In the final month of the war he served as chief of police in Prague, where he participated in the bloodless coup that led to the proclamation of an independent Czech state on

Otto Jindra in December 1916, wearing the Prussian Iron Cross Second Class in his buttonhole and five Austro-Hungarian honours on his chest (*Zdenek Cejka*)

28 October 1918. Kostrba then organised and led the Czechoslovakian Army Air Corps, but he was soon relieved of his command due to a clash of personalities with Foreign Minister Dr Edvard Benes. Kostrba rejoined the Army Air Corps as a squadron leader, but in 1926 he announced plans to leave the military to head the newly formed Czech State Airlines. On 24 September, about a week before his retirement, he took off to lead a group of Yugoslavian aircraft from Prague to Warsaw. While flying at a height of just 30 ft the lead Yugoslavian aeroplane crashed into his, killing both of its crewmen and Kostrba.

Austria-Hungary's second-ranking reconnaissance pilot was another Czech. Born in Chlumetz, Bohemia, on 18 March 1886, Otto Jindra was a career officer who also excelled in horsemanship, swimming, skiing, cycling and motoring. Graduating from the Artillery Academy in Vienna in 1905, he distinguished himself on the Russian front before declaring that he could contribute more in the LFT. On 14 September 1914 Oblt Jindra was duly assigned to *Flik* 1 as an observer, where his prior training and experience, combined with pioneering work in wireless communication by the unit's technical officer, Ltn d R Benno Fiala, helped him hone his proficiency at artillery spotting.

On 14 November Russian cavalry shot down Jindra's Albatros, but he and his pilot, Ltn Max Hesse, were unhurt. Counting 180 holes in their aeroplane, they removed whatever equipment they could carry, burned the machine and eventually made it back to friendly lines. In January 1915 *Flik* 1's CO, Oblt Josef Smetana, was taken prisoner and Jindra was named his successor.

Jindra was on a sortie in Knoller-Albatros B I 22.29, with Zgf Max Libano as his pilot, on 13 June when they were attacked by two Morane-Saulnier Parasols. Defending themselves with a Mauser pistol and a carbine, they managed to drive both Russians down in a wood near Dubovice, one force landing with the observer dead and the other crash landing, injuring both crewmen. On 27 August, Jindra, in Albatros B I 22.06 with Fw Johann Mattl, again came under attack by two Morane-Saulniers over Czortkow. Jindra's fire drove one off and forced the wounded pilot of the second to crash land near Tluste. On 1 September Jindra was promoted to hauptmann. As with Adolf Heyrowsky at *Flik* 19, his leadership nurtured talent at *Flik* 1, its future ace alumni including Fiala, Kurt Gruber, Karoly Kaszala and Godwin Brumowski. Jindra in turn began informally learning to fly, leading to his receiving the Field Pilot's Badge on 20 December.

On 5 January 1916 Jindra's Brandenburg C I 05.34 was attacked near Rarancze, resulting in a grazing wound and a bullet through the fuel tank that forced him to land. Flying Albatros B I 22.23 on 29 March, however, he scored his first success as a pilot when his observer, Kadett Franz Buchberger, sent a Parasol crash-landing at Sotal. On 4 April, again in 22.23, he and Ltn d R Vlastimil Fiala caused a Russian biplane to crash-land southeast of Kamaniec-Podolski.

On 12 April the Austro-Hungarians learned that Tsar Nicholas II was to visit Chotin. Jindra duly took off in 22.23 and arrived in time for his observer, Oblt Brumowski, to disrupt the parade with seven hand-dropped bombs. Four Morane-Saulnier Parasols intercepted the Albatros, but Brumowski drove down two.

Jindra and Oblt Eduard Struckel, in Brandenburg C I 64.23, were attacked by two Nieuports on 26 September. One of their opponents was shot in the throat by Struckel, and although the Russian pilot managed to force land, he died moments later. On 12 December Jindra, in C I 63.06, attacked a balloon near Pozoritta, his observer riddling it with 500 holes before it was pulled down with the observer dead in the basket. On 13 September 1917 Jindra's Brandenburg 67.30 was brought down by anti-aircraft fire, but he emerged unharmed.

In January 1918 Jindra was appointed commander of *Flik* 11, although he soon got a more active command in *Fliegergruppe* G when he was posted to a bombing unit on the Italian front. He was injured during a night flight shortly after his arrival, and command of the squadron had to be passed on to Jindra's old pilot from 1914, Max Hesse.

After the war Jindra helped establish the Czechoslovakian Army Air Corps, but failing health due to past injuries led him to retire in 1921. He continued to promote both the state airline and civil aviation until his death in Prague on 4 May 1932 at the age of 46.

Fellow Czech Augustin Novak was born in Batenwald and distinguished himself in the horse artillery. In January 1916 he took flight training, getting his certificate on 13 July, followed by assignment to *Flik* 30 in the Carpathians. On 12 August his Lloyd C III crashed, putting him and his observer, Oblt Egon Wagner, in hospital. With no observer willing to fly with him after his recovery, Novak was transferred to *Flik* 13 at Czik-Tapolczay, on the Rumanian front, in November.

On 27 November, during a bombing sortie to the Rumanian railway complex at Onişti in Brandenburg C I 27.01 with Ltn Alexander Souhrada of *Flik* 29 as his observer, Novak was attacked by a Farman, which was sent crashing at Brăneşti. That afternoon Novak returned to Onişti with *Flik* 13's technical officer, Ltn August Kosutic, who scored a direct bomb hit on the station. The Rumanians sent up two Farmans, but in a hard-fought action each was shot down in turn.

Novak was transferred on 30 December to newly forming *Flik* 39, where he practised his flying constantly before the unit was sent to Czeik-Szereda in March 1917. On 21 June Novak, in C I 69.53 with Rittm Karl Lukats, engaged what he called a 'large three-engined Farman' (more likely a Caudron G 4) over Comăneşti and shot it down. On 7 July, however, two Nieuports attacked him over Dărmăneşti. Badly wounded, Novak barely managed to get crippled C I 67.52 back to friendly territory, crashing near Bergy Magyaros. His observer, Ltn Ferenc Firtos von Felsöbenced, died of wounds the next day.

At the end of September *Flik* 39 was transferred to the Isonzo Front, where, on 11 November 1917, Novak and Ltn Hans Happack, in C I 129.47, downed an Italian SAML S 2 over Monte Grappa. From January 1918 Novak served as a flight instructor.

Another hero on the oft-overlooked Eastern front is Kurt Nachod, who was born on 8 March 1890 in Brünn (now Brno), Moravia. When war broke out he went from serving in the infantry to chauffeuring senior officers in Serbia to commanding an armoured railway train in northern Italy. In September 1915 he entered the LFT as an observer. In October he was assigned to *Flik* 10 in Russia, shifting to *Flik* 20 in February 1916.

Kurt Nachod as a Leutnant in der Reserve in 1915. An exceptional student, he became fluent in German, Czech, English, French and Spanish before the war (*via Aaron Weaver*)

This album photo of Fw Augustin Novak shows him with *Flik* 30 in the Carpathians in August 1916 (*via Aaron Weaver*)

Fw Gyula Busa of *Fluggeschwader* 1, seen here in January 1917, had the dual distinction of scoring five victories in two-seaters and of being one of two Hungarian aces (with Rudolf Szepessy-Sököll Freiherr von Negyes és Renö) to fall victim to Italian ace of aces Francesco Baracca (*via Aaron Weaver*)

On 31 May Ltn Nachod, in Knoller-Albatros 22.18, forced a Russian Farman to land near Klewan. On 3 July he spotted another Farman north of Luck and ordered his pilot, Zgf Franz Zuzmann, to dive at it, only to suffer a jammed machine gun. Undaunted, Nachod used a carbine to drive the enemy down for a forced landing. On 20 September he and Zgf Julius Minar, in Brandenburg C I 26.64, forced another Russian to land. On 7 January 1917 Nachod and Kpl Friedrich Camoch, in Brandenburg 26.54, drove a Nieuport and a Farman to forced landings near Luck, bringing Nachod's tally to five. In July 1917 he joined *Fluggeschwader* I on the Isonzo Front (later redesignated *Flik* 101/G of *Fliegergruppe* G) and became a pilot. While practising night landings in Brandenburg C I 269.32 on 9 May 1918, however, Nachod crashed, dying of his injuries two days later.

As with Josef Pürer, Gyula Busa, born in Budapest on 18 February 1891, was destined to fall victim to another ace. Qualifying as a pilot on 6 December 1915, he was assigned to *Flik* 14 in Russia. Flying Lloyd C II 42.45 on 23 June 1916, Busa and his observer, Kadett-Aspirant Hermann Klecker, forced two Russian biplanes to land after the latter had fired only 60 rounds.

During a long-range reconnaissance around Brody and Berstoechko on 23 November, Busa and Ltn Johann Popelak were attacked by three Russian aeroplanes, but again Busa's skilled flying and Popelak's marksmanship resulted in all three going down. Busa was promoted to feldwebel on 20 October, and five weeks later he was transferred to *Fluggeschwader* I at Divacca, on the Isonzo Front.

On 13 May 1917 Capitano Francesco Baracca of the crack *91ª Squadriglia* was patrolling with Tenente Fulco Ruffo di Calabria in their new SPAD VIIs when he reported, 'I made frontal contact with a formation of Austrian fighters. By rapid and precise fire I surprised the aircraft at the head of the enemy formation, and he fell quickly'. As Brandenburg C I 129.20 went down in flames its observer, Oblt Hermann Grössler, jumped from a height of 3000 metres – he had no parachute, but preferred that death to burning. Gyula Busa, probably already dead, crashed near Plava, his C I having become the 11th of an eventual 34 victories credited to Italy's ace of aces.

Born in Innsbrück on 28 July 1887 to a Tyrolean mother and the scion of a centuries-old line of Croatian officers, Raoul Stojsavljevic was himself a 1908 graduate of the Maria Theresa Military Academy at Wiener-Neustadt and specialised in alpine combat until 1913, when his interest shifted to aviation. When war broke out Oblt Stojsavljevic served in *Flik* 1 until November 1914, when he became deputy commander of *Flik* 13. On 15 February 1915 he and Ltn Johannes Reichel were forced down by a snowstorm just 300 yards from a Russian divisional command station. Hastily burning their aeroplane prior to being taken prisoner, they spent six days in captivity before escaping. On the run for the next four months, they hid out mostly in Lemberg (now Lviv, Ukraine) until Austro-Hungarian forces took the city on 22 June and found them.

In the late summer of 1915 Stojsavljevic was assigned to *Flik* 17 in the south Tyrol. Promoted to hauptmann on 1 September, he was transferred mid-month to *Flik* 16 at Villach, becoming CO of the unit in December. In January 1916 Ltn d R Josef Friedrich arrived. A Sudeten German born on 12 September 1893, Friedrich was an infantryman before becoming an aerial observer. He and Stojsavljevic became close friends and an equally tight team. This became evident while flying Brandenburg C I 64.14 on 4 July 1916, when they were attacked by two Italian Farmans and Friedrich holed the fuel tank of MF857, which force landed near Malborghet, its crew being taken prisoner. On the 25th they downed a second Farman after a fierce 45-minute contest. In 64.13 on 7 August they sent a third Farman crashing in the Val di Raccolana. Stojsavljevic had another observer on 1 September when they downed a Farman in the Val Dogna after a ten-minute dogfight.

In February 1917 Stojsavljevic trained in fighters and took a two-month posting in *Flik* 34, during which time, flying Brandenburg D I 65.68, he claimed a Farman south of Kostanjevica on the 13th. Soon after, however, he crashed in one of the treacherous 'Star-Strutters', suffering a knee injury that would cause him pain for the rest of his life. Back in *Flik* 16, he and Friedrich, in Brandenburg 68.11, forced a Farman to land at their airfield on 17 April, capturing both the aeroplane and its crew.

Friedrich was by then himself a pilot, having sought every opportunity to learn to fly – he had received his *Feldpilot*'s badge on 8 January 1917. On 3 May he was at the controls of Brandenburg 68.59, with Ltn Hans Rucker as observer, when they engaged a Farman that Rucker downed in the Seebach Valley after firing 50 rounds.

Also in May Stojsavljevic served a short sabbatical with *Jasta* 6 on the Western Front. His next four victories were scored in single-seaters, but his combat career ended in Brandenburg C I 68.07 on 12 January 1918 when he was attacked by enemy fighters and badly shot up (he suffered a shattered femur amongst his wounds). Nevertheless, he crossed the lines to force land in the Val Stizzone. After recovering enough to walk – against his surgeon's expectations – 'Iron Stoj' finished the war as commander of the Officers' Flight School at Wiener-Neustadt.

Meanwhile, Friedrich had also transferred, scoring two more victories in Albatros D IIIs with *Flik* 24 and serving in *Flik* 55/J from February to April 1918. Promoted to oberleutnant on 1 May 1918, he was posted to the Fighter Pilot School at Pergine in June, commenced the evaluation of new fighter types at Aspern aerodrome, near Vienna, in July and ended the war as CO of the Fighter Pilot School at Neumarkt.

Declining friends' invitations to join the new Yugoslavian state, Stojsavljevic chose to remain an Austrian, alternating between military and civilian flying endeavours before joining ÖLAG, Austria's largest commercial airline, in 1928. On 2 September 1930, while flying a Junkers F 13 alone from Innsbrück to Zürich, he encountered thick fog and crashed into a mountainside near Partenkirchen, Bavaria. He was buried in Innsbrück with every honour Austria could bestow.

Born in Mährisch-Ostrau on 30 November 1894, Andreas Dombrowski entered army service in 1915 and soon transferred into aviation, displaying a natural confidence that earned him his certificate on 17 June 1916. Assigned to *Flik* 29 at Stanislau, he was soon caught up in the Brusilov offensive. On 17 August Dombrowski's observer in Brandenburg C I 26.37, Kadettaspirant Franz Sycek, shot down a Russian Voisin after a ten-minute duel.

Switching to the Rumanian front in September, Dombrowski distinguished himself on long-range reconnaissance, bombing and

Oblt d R Josef Friedrich, shown in 1918, scored four victories as observer to Raoul Stojsavljevic, one as a two-seater pilot and two in fighters. After the war Friedrich completed his studies to become a certified engineer and was last known to be working in Rischenberg, Czechoslovakia (*via Aaron Weaver*)

A prewar aviator, Raoul Stojsavljevic had earned his pilot's certificate in Wiener-Neustadt on 7 July 1913. On 14 October he was passenger to Oblt Eugen Elsner when they flew the first Austro-Hungarian aeroplane to traverse the Alps, from Vienna to Görz (now Gorizia, Italy). He is seen here in Brandenburg D.I 28.30 of *Flik* 16 at Villach aerodrome on 14 August 1917 (*via Aaron Weaver*)

especially artillery spotting missions. On 5 February 1917 his aeroplane was attacked by a Nieuport, but his observer, Oblt Karl Patzelt, sent it crashing into a ravine west of Comăneşti. Another Nieuport attacked Dombrowski on 13 June, although once again his observer, Rittm Dr Moritz Katona de Dercsika, forced it down northwest of Oneşti. Eight days later Dombrowski and Patzelt sent another Nieuport crashing into a wood north of Borsani. Finally, on 10 July, he and Ltn d R Andreas Malitzky – a trained balloon observer new to aeroplanes – shot down what Dombrowski described as a 'three-engined large aircraft' just behind enemy lines near Soveja.

Having become an ace in two-seaters, Stfw Dombrowski was reassigned to newly formed fighter unit *Flik* 68/J in April 1918. The Italy-based unit was led by his former observer Oblt Patzelt, who was now a pilot with five victories of his own. On 4 May, however, a patrol was jumped over Vidor by RAF Camels of No 66 Sqn, which credited two Albatros D IIIs each to 2Lts Gerald A Birks and Gordon F M Apps and one to Lts Vivian S Parker and Lt William C Hilborn. *Flik* 68/J's actual losses were less in number, but grievous nevertheless – Patzelt was, in Birks' words, 'burned to a crisp', and Flugfr Franz Fritsch was also killed. Dombrowski, in Albatros 153.195, was credited with a Camel in flames for his sixth victory (although No 66 Sqn suffered no losses) before being forced to land near Piave de Soligo – probably by Apps – and miraculously surviving a strafing attack by 2Lt George D McLeod of No 28 Sqn that resulted in his face being grazed by a bullet.

Once healed, Dombrowski finished out the war at *Flik* 57/Rb, a photo-reconnaissance unit based at San Godega di Urbano airfield, with which he flew Brandenburg C Is and Phönix C Is.

A Transylvanian Saxon, Rudolf Weber was born in 1890 in Segesvár (now in Rumania) and served in the infantry, before joining *Flik* 25 as an observer in mid-April 1916. On 12 June, while flying Brandenburg C I 26.21, Weber and his pilot, Zgf Magerl, had a lengthy duel with a Voisin, Magerl contributing with his carbine to send it crashing in Russian lines. Russian anti-aircraft fire took its toll a short while later, however, when Weber suffered a shrapnel wound to the face that necessitated a long, painful convalescence in Lemberg. He had been so disfigured that he refused to be photographed thereafter. Weber also decided to take pilot training, and in the spring of 1917 he was posted to *Flik* 2 in Italy.

On the morning of 11 August Weber and Ltn d R Franz Schütz downed an Italian Nieuport, and he and Oblt Bruno Kainz claimed another that afternoon. The next day Weber and Ltn Alfons Kratochwill sent a two-seater crashing in Italian lines. On 14 September Weber was credited with his fifth success, and on 26 October he was flying single-seat Brandenburg D I 65.73 when he forced a SPAD VII to make an emergency landing near Podlensce.

In January 1918 Weber was withdrawn for a short hiatus at the *Fliegerarsenal*, after which he was appointed commander of *Flik* 102/G, a bombing unit at Aviano equipped with Brandenburg C Is and German-built Gotha G IVs. Amid the general collapse of October 1918 Weber led an aerial evacuation to Laibach (now Ljubljana, in Slovenia), where *Flik* 102/G's aeroplanes were confiscated by the new Yugoslav government. Weber and some comrades resumed the trek homeward in a commandeered automobile, but at a roadside checkpoint in Styria he was mistakenly shot and killed by a member of the Austrian volunteer militia. His remains were interred in the Central Cemetery in Vienna.

Fellow ace Frantisek (Franz) Wognar was born in Nagyszombat, Hungary, on 6 January 1890, although he was of Slovak descent. A skilled mechanic, he enlisted in the army in 1913 and opted for pilot training the following year. In July 1915 he was assigned to *Flik* 2 on the Isonzo Front, where he flew a variety of missions in an equally wide variety of two-seaters. On 26 January 1917 Wognar and Kadettaspirant Josef Matijevic, in Brandenburg C I 29.75, forced a Nieuport down in Italian lines. On 1 May he and Ltn Silvius Frimmel claimed another Nieuport, but on the 20th Wognar's C I 229.20 was jumped over Monte Sabotino by a SPAD VII. He was wounded in the back before his Hungarian observer, Ltn Ferenc Gräser, could drive the fighter down to force land in Italian lines. Wognar's third victory was Gräser's second of an eventual 18, the rest being scored as a fighter pilot prior his death in action on 17 May 1918.

After only ten days' hospitalisation Wognar was back at *Flik* 2, and on 4 September he was credited with his fourth victory. Twelve days later he was asked to eliminate an Italian balloon operating near Liga, and flying Brandenburg C I 29.69 he dove on it firing, after which his observer, Ltn d R Otto Patz, loosed a parting volley that set it ablaze.

In late December 1917 Wognar was withdrawn from the frontline and subsequently served as a test pilot. In 1918 he married a Slovenian girl and had risen to the rank of offizierstellvertreter by war's end.

Korporal Franz Wognar poses beside a Knoller-Albatros B I in 1915. Although born in Hungary, 'Frantisek' Wognar was of Slovak extraction. Details of his life after the Hapsburg Empire's dissolution – and under which nationality he chose to live it – are unknown, but he was reported to have died in Odessa in 1943, possibly as an Axis prisoner of war in Soviet hands *(via Aaron Weaver)*

APPENDICES

Reconnaissance and Bomber Pilot Aces of the RFC, RNAS and RAF

Pilot	Sqn(s)	Score
E D Asbury	49	5
L A Ashfield	202	5
R N G Atkinson	10, 98, 206	5
R L M Barbour	205	6
C P O Bartlett	5N	8
J D Belgrave	45, 61, 60	6 (total 18)
C Bowman	49	6
D H M Carbery	52, 59	6
R Chalmers	205	6
W H Clarke	205	5
G H Cock	45	13
G W F Darville	18	9
E Dickson	10N, 5N, 205	14
R E Dodds	106, 103	7
A T Drinkwater	57, 40	9
D E Edgley	57	6
W B Elliott	103, 205	5
G Fox-Rule	49	7
M B Frew	45	5 (total 23)
R J Gammon	104	5
J Gamon	5N, 205	7
J G Gillanders	18	5
H R Gould	18	6
W E Green	57	9
W Grossart	205	5
D S Hall	57	6
H R Harker	57	5
C J Heywood	5N, 205	6
J B Hume-Hay	104	7
O C W Johnsen	98	5
E G Joy	49, 57, 205	8
J A Keating	49	6
N Keeble	1W(N), 2N, 202	6
C T Lally	25	5
T F Le Mesurier	5N, 11N	7
C R Lupton	5N, 205	5
A MacGregor	57	5
L Minot	16, 57	6
J F Morris	25	7
P H O'Lieff	1, 55	5
L H Pearson	2N, 202	6
C R Pithey	12	10
J E Pugh	25	5
A Roulstone	25, 57	8
G H B Smith	104	5
A R Spurling	49	6
D A Stewart	20, 18	16
C H Stokes	57	5
J S Stubbs	103	11
F M C Turner	55, 57	7
A G Waller	18	11
L R Warren	6N, 206	8
F C Wilton	98	6

Reconnaissance and Bomber Observer Aces of the RFC, RNAS and RAF

Observer	Sqn(s)	Score
P E Appleby	104	6
F W Bell	9, 49	6
E B C Betts	2N, 202	6
B J Blackett	25, 18	5
G N Blennerhassett	18	8
C C Blizard	104	5
W E Bottrill	104	5
A F Britton	57	6
D L Burgess	25	7
L A Christian	6N, 206	9
L I Collins	18	5
I B Corey	103	6
L S Court	25	8
F G Craig	57	5
C C Dance	103	6
E Darby	5N, 202	6
W N Dyke	18	5
C E Eddy	103	5
L H Emsden	25	8
H C T Gompertz	55	5
J Grant	57	8
S H Hamblin	205	6
T M Harries	45, 24	6 (total 11)
C P Harrison	98	5
W Harrop	104	5
E P Hartigan	57	5
P T Holligan	49	6
H S Jackson	5N	6
W Jones	205	6
M B Kilroy	18	5
S F Langstone	5N, 205	5
F Leathley	57	8
H W M Mackay	18	5
F T S Menendez	57	6
W J Middleton	5N, 205	6
W Miller	18	6
W Naylor	5N	14
H Pullen	18	5
A B Rattray	104	5
H Rhodes	12	11
C V Robinson	5N, 205	7
W H Scott	5N, 205	8
E A Simpson	49	6
L L T Sloot	57	5
J R Smith	18	5
W T Smith	45, 104	5
E Walker	18	6
C M Witham	205	5

French Reconnaissance and Bomber Pilot Aces

Pilot	*Escadrille(s)*	Score
Paul Constant Homo	C202, C225, Br235	5
Jean Jannekeyn	Br132	5
Didier Lecour-Grandmaison	R46	5
Jean Loste	R46	7
Albert Edmond Mézergue	Sop123, Br131	7
Antoine Paillard	Sop111, Br132	5
Joseph Vuillemin	C11, *Escadre* 12	7

French Reconnaissance and Bomber Observer Aces

Observer	*Escadrille(s)*	Score
Charles A B Borzecki	N3, N62	5
Alexandre Buisson	Br29, R240	5
Adolphe du Bois d'Aische	F71	6
Louis H Martin	R46	6
Achille J E Rousseaux	R46	6
Léon G F M Vitalis	R46	7
Eugène Weismann	Br132	7

Austro-Hungarian Reconnaissance Pilot Aces

Pilot	*Fliegerkompagnie*	Two-seater Score	Total
Adolf Heyrowsky	9, 19	11	12
Otto Jindra	1	9	9
Julius Arigi	6, FIG1, 55J, 6F, 1F	7	32
István Fejes	19, 51J	5	16
Raoul Stojsavljevic	1, 13, 17, 16, 34	5	10
Jindrich Kostrba ze Skalice	4, 23	5	8
Sandor Tahy	19, 51J	5	8
Josef Friedrich	16, 24, 55J	5	7
Otto Jäger	10, 27, 42J	5	7
Andreas Dombrowski	29, 68J	5	6
Rudolf Weber	25, 2	5	6
Gyula Busa	14	5	5
Augustin Novak	13, 39, 39D	5	5
Franz Wognar	2	5	5

Austro-Hungarian Reconnaissance Observer Aces

Observer	*Fliegerkompagnie*	Two-seater score	Total
János Frint	23	6	6
Johann Lasi	6, Flek 6	5	5
Kurt Nachod	20	5	5

COLOUR PLATES

Artist Harry Dempsey has created the colour profiles for this volume, working closely with the author to portray the aircraft as accurately as circumstances permit. Some of the illustrations are, admittedly, reconstructions based on fragmentary photographic evidence or descriptions provided by the pilots while they were alive, combined with known unit marking policy.

1

Caudron G 4 (serial unknown) of Capt Joseph Vuillemin and Lt Paul Moulines, C11, Ancemont-sur-Meuse, France, March 1916

Capt Joseph Vuillemin introduced his red cocotte emblem flying Caudron G 4s with C11, which also appeared on Nieuport 11 N1313 that was issued to him for escorting the reconnaissance aeroplanes in the unit. Vuillemin and Lt Paul Moulines were in a Caudron, however, when they brought down a Fokker Eindecker over Marcheville-en-Woëvre. This was Vuillemin's second confirmed victory. Although the cocotte was duly adopted as C11's unit insignia, Vuillemin continued to use it as a personal motif on his Breguet 14B2 when he led *Escadre* 12 on bombing missions in 1918, during which time he scored four more victories to bring his confirmed total to seven.

2

Sopwith 1A2 N° 6 of Sgt Gabriel Hébert and Adj Charles Borzecki, N62, Chipilly, France, November 1916

One of three 1½ Strutters used by N62 for long-range photo-reconnaissance missions in late 1916, this Sopwith-built aeroplane was on a mission encompassing Allaines, Aizecourt-le-Haut, Templeux-la-Fosse, Nurlu and Ytres on 23 November when it was attacked by eight German two-seaters. Adj Borzecki sent one of the enemy machines crashing to earth near Ytres for his third of five victories, and a second German aeroplane was downed at Bus by his squadronmate Lt Pierre Lhuillier, who was escorting the Sopwith in Nieuport 17 N1665. Hébert and Borzecki would share in another success while flying Hanriot-built Sopwith N° 22 on 10 February 1917.

3

Dorand AR 1 N° 1261 of Cpl Henri Bétis and Sgt Adolphe du Bois d'Aische, AR71, Sainte-Ménehould, France, July 1917

On 24 July 1917 four AR 1s of AR71 were on a reconnaissance mission when they came under attack from nine Albatros scouts, which drove two of the aeroplanes down in French lines. Sgt Adolphe Couture was killed and Adj Roger Pons wounded in one of the machines. The other AR 1, crewed by Cpl Bétis and Sgt du Bois d'Aische, shot down two of its assailants over Cerny-en-Dormois before crashing. Bétis died of his wounds on the 27th, but du Bois d'Aische was unhurt. These were the third and fourth victories of an eventual six credited to du Bois d'Aische. Both ARs crash-landed too far within their own lines for *Jasta* 9 to get any confirmations for its trouble, the unit having had Ltn Oskar Dankert killed in action during the engagement at Pont-à-Chin.

4

Caudron R 4 (serial unknown) of Capt Didier Lecour-Grandmaison, Sous-Lt Pierre Arthur and MdL Léon Vitalis, R46, Demuin, France, September 1916

MdL Léon Vitalis was photographed in the rear gunner's cockpit of this death's head marked Caudron R 4, suggesting that it was Capt Lecour-Grandmaison's prior to Vitalis' move up to the front observer's position on 10 November 1916, when the latter scored his fifth victory (and Lecour-Grandmaison's fourth) of an eventual seven.

5

Caudron R 4 (serial unknown) of Sgt Étienne Combret and Brigs Achille Rousseaux and Georges Cadot, R46, Demuin, France, September 1916

Achille Rousseaux was photographed near this decorative Caudron, possibly after driving an enemy aeroplane down in German lines in collaboration with Capt Lecour-Grandmaison, Sous-Lt Arthur and MdL Vitalis, on 8 September 1916. This would be the first of an eventual six victories for Rousseaux.

6

Letord 1 (serial unknown) of Capt Didier Lecour-Grandmaison, Cpl Joseph Crozet and Sgt Alfred Boyé, Let46, Bonnemaison-Lhéry, France, May 1917

Letord 1 N° 10 is believed to have been normally crewed by Lt Marcel Bloch and Sgts Léonard Joussen and Alfred Boyé, but it was being flown by Let46's CO, with Cpl Joseph Crozet and Boyé, on 10 May 1917 when it was attacked by Albatros D Vs of *Jasta* 15 and shot down in French lines by the *Staffelführer*, Ltn Heinrich Gontermann. Lecour-Grandmaison and Crozet were killed, but the wounded Boyé gained enough control to bring the aeroplane out of its spin, cross into French lines and miraculously survive the crash landing.

7

Caudron R 11 N° 6514 of R240, Matouges, France, October 1918

Largely due to the remarkable victory tally racked up by the Caudron R 4 and Letord 1 aircrews of R46 in 1916, the French began using the Caudron R 11s of that and other units as fighter escorts for Breguet 14B2 bombers in 1918. One of the newer such *escadrilles*, R240, produced at least one ace gunner, Adj Alexandre Buisson, who had scored his first success in a Farman with F29 followed by four with R240. Another gunner, Sgt André Coolen, was credited with at least three Germans while serving with the unit. Shown here is a typical Caudron displaying the squadron insignia of a three-headed hydra within a red ellipse and the commander's number 1. The latter means that this machine was probably flown by Capt Jehan de Durat, who, though not an ace, was made a *Chevalier de la Légion d'Honneur* on 23 October 1917 and survived the war with the *Croix de Guerre* and four palms, one gilt star, one silver star and three bronze stars. At the time of his death on 12 July 1940 – in a motorcycle accident – de Durat was a lieutenant colonel in the *Armée de l'Air* and a *Commandeur de la Légion d'Honneur*.

8

Sopwith 1B1 N° 115 of Adj Antoine Paillard, Sop111, Villeneuve-les-Vertus, France, July 1917

A Hanriot-built single-seat bomber, N° 115 bore the swan insignia of Sop111, and had a hand-applied camouflage scheme over its rear fuselage and wings. Sop 111's single-seat Sopwith 1B1s were usually unarmed, escorted by its armed 1A2 two-seaters, but Adj Antoine Paillard, already exhibiting an aggressive streak, mounted a Lewis gun above the upper wing of his bomber. During the second of two audacious night bombing missions Paillard strayed into Dutch airspace and engine trouble forced him to land at Meylum. The Sopwith was pressed into Dutch service as LA45, with orange discs and rudder, but retaining the swan motif. Paillard escaped internment on 4 November, and after returning to France he flew Breguet 14B2s in Br132, scoring five victories in May and September 1918.

9

Breguet 14B2 N° 4070 of Capt Albert Mézergues and MdL Henri Miclet, Br131, Villeneuve-le-Roi, France, June 1918

Michelin-built 14B2 N° 4070 was one of a batch produced with their factory-applied camouflage patterns in mirror image to the norm. On 25 June Capt Mézergues scored his fifth victory in concert with MdL Henri Miclet. However, shortly thereafter, they themselves came down in Allied lines, with Mézergues wounded and his observer dead. They had probably fallen victim to – and may in turn have driven down – Ltn Hans-Joachim Borck of *Jasta* 15, who was credited with a Breguet south of Rony-le-Grand.

10

Breguet 14B2 N° 4231 of Capt Jean-François Jannekeyn and Sous-Lt Eugène Weismann, Br132, Le Mensil-Amerlot, France, August 1918

Normally flown by Lt Louis Gros (four victories) and Adj Louis Laserre (three), who scored in it on 15 July 1918, this Breguet was also photographed with Capt Jean-François Jannekeyn and Sous-Lt Eugène Weisman, possibly on the occasion of their driving an enemy fighter down damaged and out of control on 22 August. The two got their next four in a single gruelling 45-minute action near Conflans on 14 September, as Br132 fought Fokker D VIIs of *Jasta* 13 and a strong headwind. Among those also credited in the joint victories were Sous-Lt Antoine Paillard and his bombardier, Sgt René Hincelin.

11

RE 8 F6097 of Lts Croye Rothes Pithey and Hervey Rhodes, No 12 Sqn, Sombrin, France, September 1918

The highest-scoring RE 8 team claimed their last three victories in this aeroplane – a DFW C V on 28 August 1918, a Fokker D VII two days later and an LVG on 3 September. Their run of luck ended when both were wounded by groundfire on 27 September. Rhodes did not fully recover until 1921, by which time Pithey had died in a crash on 21 February 1920.

12

Sopwith 1½ Strutter A8226 of Lt Geoffrey H Cock and 2Lt Allan S Carey, No 45 Sqn, Sainte-Marie-Cappel, May 1917

Lt G H Cock and 2Lt A S Carey were flying this Sopwith, resplendent in the red and white markings of 'C' Flight, when they downed an Albatros D III OOC near Lille – this was Cock's fifth victory. Capt Christopher H Jenkins was mortally wounded in the same action and Cock, besides receiving the MC, replaced him as 'B' Flight leader. Among the white-wheeled 'B' Flight Sopwiths that he flew was A1016, in which he was credited with victories on 27 May, 16 June and 6 and 13 July, with different observers on each occasion. Lt Joseph Senior was mortally wounded aboard A8226 on 9 May, and on 27 May the aeroplane was shot down by Offz Stv Max Müller of *Jasta* 28, killing Capt Lawrence W McArthur, then 'C' Flight leader, and 2Lt Carey.

13

DH 4 N5967 of Flt Lt C P O Bartlett and AGL S D Sambrook, 5 Naval Squadron, Petite-Synthe, France, July 1917

Flt Lt Charles Philip Oldfield Bartlett scored his first of eight accredited victories in N5967 during a bombing raid on Zeebrugge on 2 July 1917 when his bombardier, AGL S D Sambrook, drove an Albatros D V down out of control at 1230 hrs.

14

DH 4 A7543 of Lt Frederick Libby and 2Lt D M Hills, No 25 Sqn, Auchel, France, August 1917

A cowboy from Colorado who passed himself off as Canadian to join the RFC, Fred Libby scored ten victories as an observer in FE 2bs with Nos 23 and 11 Sqns in 1916. He then became a pilot in Sopwith 1½ Strutters with No 43 Sqn from 7 March 1917, adding enemy aeroplanes to his tally on 6 May and 23 July. He then led 'B' Flight in No 25 Sqn, and his DH 4 from this period is reconstructed with the appropriate letter for that status. Flying A7543, with 2Lt D M Hills as his observer-gunner, Libby shared the credit in driving an Albatros D V down OOC over Henin-Liétard on 8 August and a two-seater OOC over Lens six days later. He transferred into the USAS on 15 September, but was partially crippled by spondylitis shortly thereafter and saw no further combat.

15

DH 4 A7568 of Capt David S Hall and 2Lt Edward P Hartigan, No 57 Sqn, Boisdinghem, France, October 1917

DH 4 A7568 was flown by Capt David Sidney Hall, who led 'A' Flight. Hailing from Helensburgh, Scotland, and serving in the 9th Argyll and Sutherland Highlanders prior to joining the RFC, Hall, with his bombardier 2Lt N M Pizey, was credited with an Albatros D V over the Houthulst Forest on 27 July 1917. He then teamed up with 22-year-old Irishman 2Lt Edward Patrick Hartigan from Reens, County Limerick, formerly of the Royal Munster Fusiliers. On 2 October No 57 Sqn was attacked over Roulers by *Jasta* 18, losing three aeroplanes and five crewmen dead and one captured. Hall and Hartigan, however, fought their way out, and each was credited with shooting down two assailants for a shared total of four. The only German casualty, however, was Ltn Walter Kleffel, who was wounded. On 28 October the duo drove an Albatros down OOC west of Roulers, but on 20 November they failed to return from a morning sortie, and the wreckage of A7568 was later found at Les Alleux. Hall, dead at 25, was gazetted for the MC on 6 April 1918.

16

DH 4 D8402 of Lts Lionel A Ashfield and Frederick S Russell, No 202 Sqn, Bergues, France, May 1918

Born in Wootton Bassett, Wiltshire, on 1 August 1898, Lionel Arthur Ashfield studied at nearby Marlborough College until he joined the RNAS on 29 April 1917. On 15 November he joined 2 Naval Squadron, which became No 202 Sqn within the newly created RAF on 1 April 1918. In addition to 62 sorties and 17 combats, for which he received the DFC, Ashfield was credited with five victories, including an enemy aeroplane OOC over Ostende on 31 May while flying D8402 with Lt Frederick Stratton Russell as his bombardier. Ashfield usually flew A7868, and he and Lt Maurice Graham English were killed in it when the aeroplane crashed near Zevekote on 16 July after being attacked by ace Vzfmstr Hans Goerth of *Marine Feld Jasta* (MFJ) III. D8402 was being flown by USAS pilot 1Lt Walter P Chalaire and Acting Gunlayer Pte1 A E Humphreys on 29 July when it and DH 4 A7632 were attacked by seven Fokkers south of Oudekapelle. D8402 was badly shot up and subsequently dismantled after its wounded crew managed to land in Allied lines at Roesbrugge railhead, claiming two assailants OOC. Their demise were credited to Ltn z S Theo Osterkamp of MFJ II.

17

DH 9 C6114 of Lts Allan H Curtis and Philip T Holligan, No 49 Sqn, Petite-Synthe, France, April 1918

Born on 20 May 1898, Philip Terence Holligan studied at the University of Manchester School of Technology in 1915-16 and then joined the 9th Officer Cadet Battalion. He subsequently entered the RFC, being posted to No 49 Sqn on 11 December 1916. As bombardier for 2Lt Gordon Fox-Rule in DH 4 A7705, he was credited with a Rumpler on 8 March 1918 and an LVG the next day. On 23 April Holligan was in C6114, with Lt Allan Harper Curtis as his pilot, when he downed an Albatros D Va east of Nieuport. Holligan was in D3052, with Capt Clifford Bowman as his pilot, when he was credited with a Fokker D VII on 8 August, and two more the next day. Gazetted for the DFC on 2 November after having completed 50 bombing and photo-reconnaissance missions, Holligan left the RAF on 1 February 1919. C6114 was brought down in Allied lines by a Fokker D VII of *Jasta* 15 on 7 June 1918, Lt Curtis and Sgt A W Davies surviving unhurt.

18

DH 9 E8884 of Capt Roy E Dodds and 2Lt Irving B Corey, No 103 Sqn, Ronchin, France, October 1918

Provisionally reconstructed in the markings of the lead aeroplane in No 103 Sqn's 'C' Flight, E8884 was being flown by Capt Roy Edward Dodds and 2Lt Irving Benfield Corey when they drove a Fokker D VII down OOC over Mainvault on 30 October 1918 for their seventh victory.

19

DH 9 D550 of Capt John S Stubbs and 2Lt Gilbert G Bannerman, No 103 Sqn, Ronchin, France, October 1918

After previous service in No 27 Sqn until he was wounded on 9 May 1917, Capt John S Stubbs scored his 11th, and last, victory (a Fokker D VII destroyed near Montreuil) while flying D550 on 30 October. He and 2Lt Gilbert Bannerman were themselves brought down in Allied lines shortly thereafter, their demise possibly being credited to Flgmt Wasserthal of MFJ IV. Gazetted for the DFC and the Air Force Cross on 2 November, Stubbs was posted out of the unit six days later. Lt Ronald W Jackson, who replaced him in command of 'B' Flight, was flying D550 with 2Lt Edward A Slater when it was written off during a heavy landing at Ronchin on 6 January 1919.

20 and Back Cover

Salmson 2A2 N° 1984 *Jo. 4.* of Capt William T Erwin and 1Lt Arthur A Easterbrook, 1st Aero Squadron, Remicourt, France, October 1918

The last Salmson to be operationally flown by Capt Bill Erwin arrived at Remicourt on 30 September 1918. He scored his third victory – and observer 1Lt Arthur Easterbrook's first – on 6 October, and the duo downed two two-seaters on the 8th. 1Lt Byrne V Baucom was in the back seat to help down a Rumpler over Thénorgues on 15 October and a Fokker D VII over Sommerance three days later. Finally, Erwin and Easterbrook used the aeroplane to down a two-seater northwest of Remonville on 22 October. *Jo. 4.* was brought down by groundfire near Stenay on 5 November, although it was soon repaired and still on strength with the unit at Coblenz in early 1919.

21

Salmson 2A2 (serial unknown) of Capt Everett R Cook and 2Lt William T Badham, 91st Aero Squadron, Gondreville-sur-Meuse, October 1918

This Hanriot-built 2A2 was photographed with Capt Everett Cook after the war, showing his score in the form of five crosses on the knight's shield.

22

Salmson 2A2 N° 5192 of 1Lt Victor H Strahm and 1Lt Thomas M Jervey, 91st Aero Squadron, Gondreville-sur-Meuse, November 1918.

This Salmson is known to have been flown by 1Lts Victor Strahm from 5 August 1918, and was probably flown by him on 4 September 1918, when he and his observer, 'Cap' Wallis, drove down a Pfalz D IIIa, probably wounding Vfw Alfred Bäder of *Jasta* 65. Strahm's fourth and fifth victories, however, were scored with 1Lt Tom Jervey, the 91st Aero squadron's ordnance officer, volunteering to man the observer's pit on 31 October and 4 November.

23

Roland C II (serial unknown) of Vfw Fritz Kosmahl and Oblt d L Josef Neubürger, FFA 22, Cambrai, France, 1916

Vfw Fritz Kosmahl joined *Feldflieger Abteilung* 22 on 11 January 1915, and he was credited with bringing down two enemy aircraft sometime in 1916, probably flying LVG C IIs. His third victory, scored with Oblt der Landwehr Josef Neubürger on 10 October, was FE 2b 4292 of No 25 Sqn that was engaged on a bombing raid on Oppy when it was shot up by Ltn Manfred von Richthofen of *Jasta* 2 and finished off by the two-seater crew. The observer, Lt Moreton Hayne, was killed, while the pilot, 2Lt Arthur H M Copeland, was taken prisoner. Serving on after Fl Abt 22 was redesignated as artillery spotting unit Fl Abt (A) 261, the recently promoted Offz Stv Kosmahl and Ltn d R Schulz, now flying in an Albatros C V, brought down a Sopwith Pup over Hermies on 2 February 1917, killing Flt Lt Walter E Traynor of 8 Naval Squadron. On 11 March Kosmahl, again with Neubürger in the back seat, brought down an FE 2b of No 23 Sqn south of Beugny. Credited with five victories, Kosmahl subsequently became a fighter pilot, scoring four more victories with *Jasta* 26 before being shot in the stomach during a fight with SE 5as of No 60 Sqn on 22 September. He succumbed to his wounds in hospital four days later.

24

Albatros C V/16 C1220/16 of Ltn Albert Dossenbach and Oblt Hans Schilling, Fl Abt 22, Cambrai, France, late 1916

The Albatros C V differed from previous models in being built around the new 220 hp Mercedes D IV eight cylinder water-cooled engine, enclosed under a long, streamlined cowling. Heavy controls led to a redesign with balanced ailerons and elevator, as well as replacing the 'ear' radiators with one flush on the upper wing – this variant was designated C V/17 to distinguish it from the older C V/16. Although capable of 110 mph (170 kph), a climb rate of 410 feet per minute (2.1 metres per second) and a ceiling of 9840 ft (3000 m), and able to carry up to 400 lb (180 kg) of bombs, the C V was undone by its chronically malfunctioning engine, which caused production to cease after the construction of just 400 aeroplanes. It is not known how many victories – if any – Ltn Albert Dossenbach and Oblt Hans Schilling scored in C V/16 C 1220/16, but Dossenbach was photographed beside it, and apparently had it customised with a pointier airscrew spinner. Dossenbach's score stood at nine when he received the *Orden Pour le Mérite* on 11 November 1916, becoming the first two-seater pilot so honoured. Going on to fighters with *Jasta* 2, he scored five victories as leader of *Jasta* 36 and then burned a balloon as commander of *Jasta* 10. On 3 July 1917, however, Dossenbach was shot down and killed – ironically by DH 4 crew Capt Laurence Minot and Lt A F Brown of No 57 Sqn.

25

Hannover CL IIIa 2622/18 of Gfr Johann Baur and Ltn Georg Hengl, Fl Abt (A) 295b, Montigny-le-Franc, France, August 1918

Born near Mühldorf on 24 April 1897, Johann Baur was assigned to Royal Bavarian Fl Abt (A) 295 and was credited with six victories during the course of 160 missions. His regular observer, Ltn Hengl, scored a seventh victory while with another pilot and acquired the noble title of Georg von Hengl after the war.

26

Knoller-Albatros B I 22.23 of Oblts Otto Jindra and Godwin Brumowski, *Flik* 1, Zastava, Bukovina, April 1916

On 12 April 1916 the Austro-Hungarians learned that Tsar Nicholas II was to visit Russian army headquarters at Chotin for a formal reception. Keen to disrupt the festivities, *Flik* 1's commander, Oblt Otto Jindra, took off in B I 22.23 and arrived just as the parade was getting underway, at which point his observer, Oblt Godwin Brumowski, hand dropped seven bombs that caused a satisfying amount of chaos. Four Morane-Saulnier Parasols intercepted the party crashers, but Brumowski's accurate gunfire sent two down to crash land, with one pilot severely wounded and two crewmen injured. The tsar was furious, but Gen Aleksei A Brusilov, ever the professional, gave the sortie its due as 'an extraordinarily bold and courageous deed by the Austrian fliers'. Jindra survived the war with nine victories, while Brumowski switched to fighters and became Austria-Hungary's ace of aces with a total of 35.

27

Hansa-Brandenburg C I 61.64. of StFw Julius Arigi and Fw Johann Lasi, *Flik* 6, Kavaja, Albania, August 1916

Built in Germany, as indicated by the second period in its serial number, C I 61.64. was serving with a detachment from *Flik* 6 at Kavaja, south of the unit's main airfield at Skutari, in Albania, on 22 August 1916 when it intercepted six Farmans of the Italian *34ª Squadriglia*. The crew of StFw Julius Arigi and Fw Johann Lasi claimed no fewer than five of them. On 4 September Arigi, still in 61.64. with Ltn Fabian Lukas-Sluja in the observer's pit, brought down another Farman at Fjeri. The aeroplane's unidentified pilot and his observer, Capt Dr Fausto Pesci, CO of *34ª Squadriglia* and one of Arigi's 'victims' of 22 August, were taken prisoner. On 18 September Arigi and Kadett Viktor Karl Renvez, again in 61.64., forced a Caproni bomber to land at Arta Terme, just behind Italian lines.

28

Hansa-Brandenburg C I 29.64 of Hptm Adolf Heyrowski, *Flik* 19, Ghirano, Italy, September 1917

License-built by Phönix, C I 29.64 was delivered to *Flik* 19 in early 1917 and flown by Heyrowski from April through to September, during which time he used it to claim five of his twelve victories. The aeroplane was also crewed on occasion by aces Ludwig Hautzmeyer and Josef Pürer. In the autumn of 1917 its upper flying surfaces, fuselage and wheels were given the splotched camouflage pattern depicted here, which was applied with rags or sponges saturated with brown paint. The white and red band was a *Flik* 19 marking.

BIBLIOGRAPHY

Bailey, Frank W and Cony, Christophe, *The French Air Service War Chronology, 1914-1918*, Grub Street, London, 2001
Bowyer, Chaz, *For Valour – The Air VCs*, Grub Street, London, 1992
Franks, Norman, *Sharks Among Minnows*, Grub Street, London, 2001
Franks, Norman, Bailey, Frank and Duivan, Rick, *The Jasta War Chronology*, Grub Street, London, 1998
Franks, Norman, 'Pithey & Rhodes – RE 8 Team', *Cross & Cockade Great Britain Journal*, Vol 4, No 3, 1973, pp 114-117
Jefford, Wg Cdr C G, *The Flying Camels – The History of No 45 Sqn, RAF*, Unwin Bros Ltd, Old Woking, Surrey, 1995
Kilduff, Peter, *Richthofen – Beyond the Legend of the Red Baron*, Arms & Armour Press, London, 1993
Libby, Frederick, *Horses Don't Fly – A Memoir of World War I*, Arcade Publishing, New York, 2000
Martel, René, translated and edited by Allan Suddaby, *French Strategic and Tactical Bombardment Forces of World War I*, Scarecrow Press, Lanham, Maryland, 2007
O'Connor, Dr Martin, *Air Aces of the Austro-Hungarian Empire 1914-1918*, Champlin Fighter Museum Press, Mesa, Arizona, 1986
Rennles, Keith, *Independent Force*, Grub Street, London, 2002
Shores, Christopher, Franks, Norman and Guest, Russell, *Above the Trenches*, Grub Street, London, 1990

INDEX

References to illustrations are shown in **bold**. Plates are shown with page and caption locators in brackets.